ED ROBB

MAKING ROOM

SHARING THE LOVE OF CHRISTMAS

Abingdon Press | Nashville

MAKING ROOM
Sharing the Love of Christmas

Library of Congress Control Number: 2020938769
ISBN-13: 978-1-7910-0637-2

20 21 22 23 24 25 26 27 28 29—10 9 8 7 6 5 4 3 2 1
MANUFACTURED IN THE UNITED STATES OF AMERICA

To my parents
who loved me into faith

CONTENTS

INTRODUCTION

Perhaps your family, like mine, either read the book or watched the animated version of Dr. Seuss's classic story *How the Grinch Stole Christmas!* every Christmas season. Our children—and grandchildren—were fascinated with the lonely, cantankerous, green-colored outcast, who lived on a frigid mountaintop far above the town of Whoville. It's an imaginative story, and for me, the most memorable part comes at the end. The Grinch, seated at a long table with the entire Whoville community, is given the honor of carving the roast beast. His smile reveals his genuine delight in being warmly welcomed into the midst of their community feast.

The story's imagery transports me back to a community table I delighted in visiting during my childhood: the fellowship hall of my grandparents' church. Theirs was a small, rural Methodist church in Texas. The kind of small where everyone knew each other by name. The kind of small where visits and meals were immediately put into action when Mrs. Jones was admitted to the hospital. The kind of small where volunteers were quickly recruited to help Mr. Smith plow his field after his tractor broke down. The kind of small where, every five years, pastors were lovingly prayed over as they left for new assignments and where incoming pastors were warmly welcomed with, of course, a potluck dinner.

Sunday worship was an event we looked forward to all week long. Grandmother made sure we looked our very best before we piled into the car to head for church. Getting there early was the rule because it afforded us the time to connect with friends before the service began. And after the service, the entire church community headed to the fellowship hall. What great fun we had, racing up and down the hall between the tables with the friends we had made on our visits. While our grandparents got caught up on all the community news, we snagged enough doughnuts and cookies to power our sugar-energy reserves for an entire afternoon.

Food was never in short supply at that Methodist church's fellowship hall. Potluck dinners were a regular event featuring culinary delights such as southern fried chicken, funeral potatoes, calico beans, fried okra, and blue-ribbon-winning brown-sugar-cinnamon apple pie. Also served up were healthy portions of love, laughter, and fellowship.

Looking back, the fellowship hall seemed to me to be twice as large as the church's sanctuary. But that's not surprising really since it held the heart and spirit of Christian community within its walls.

I often think of my grandparents' church as I read through the early chapters of the Acts of the Apostles, because small churches like theirs captured many of the dynamics of the earliest Christian church, which was born through the giving of Holy Spirit at Pentecost. This is what Acts 2:42-47 tells us about the fellowship of believers in Jerusalem:

> *They devoted themselves to the apostles' teaching and to fellowship, to the breaking of bread and to prayer. Everyone was filled with awe at the many wonders and signs*

performed by the apostles. All the believers were together and had everything in common. They sold property and possessions to give to anyone who had need. Every day they continued to meet together in the temple courts. They broke bread in their homes and ate together with glad and sincere hearts, praising God and enjoying the favor of all the people. And the Lord added to their number daily those who were being saved.

The word *fellowship* comes from the Greek *koinonia*, meaning "community." Fellowship includes two important elements: deepening friendship and developing a common vision, goals, and priorities. In the first-century church, fellowship was mediated by meals, an important tradition of Jewish Christians. Meals would always begin with a blessing over bread, as a remembrance of God's provision for the meal, and then breaking and sharing it. (Jesus understood and observed this practice and added additional meaning to the act of breaking bread at the Last Supper with his disciples. His words from Matthew—"Take and eat; this is my body" [26:26] and "This is my blood of the covenant, which is poured out for many for the forgiveness of sins" [26:28]—expressed what he would provide with the breaking, death, and resurrection of his body.) After the breaking of the bread during those early church meals, the remainder of the time would be devoted to fellowship and encouraging one another in living the life God wants us to live.[1]

This intimate, communal love for God and one another is the glue that held the early church together and is what I observed and experienced in the small-town and rural churches of my youth. But as our cities have grown and expanded into the masses of suburbia, I fear we are losing that glue. Some churches are growing larger and larger, offering many different worship times and venues. Worshipers must be in and out in an hour to make room for the next service, leaving little time for fellowship. Rare are the congregations where members know all the others by name.

The church I serve near Houston, Texas, The Woodlands United Methodist Church, has fourteen thousand members. It's a big church with thirteen ordained clergy and a large staff. So many people attend on any given Sunday that a worshiper can easily get lost or overwhelmed. More and more I have come to realize that it doesn't matter how many programs or how many square feet of space we have if we aren't successful in getting members into small groups where they come to know one another and share a sense of community. In time, members are likely to become inactive, marginalized, and disillusioned.

We cannot grow as Christians while living in isolation since faith is always communal. This is not a new idea. John Wesley, the founder of the Methodist movement within the Church of England, believed that "the gospel of Christ knows of no religion, but social; no holiness but social holiness." Wesley scholar Steve Manskar explains:

> *[Wesley believed that] holiness is social because God is social. He created human beings in his image to be relational creatures. We become fully human when we share in the relationships God initiates with us through the people he places in our way....If you truly love God then you must love your brother and sister in Christ and your neighbor. This requires you to be in relationships with the people God*

places alongside you in the church, and the people of your neighborhood, city, and the world. You need community, what Wesley called "society," for grace to nurture you into the persons God created you to be.[2]

"[John Wesley's] development of small groups revolutionized 18th century England and provided a framework to help people grow in 'holiness of heart and life,'" the magazine *Holiness Today* says. "Small groups provided a context in which seekers could receive support, accountability, and encouragement."[3]

Jesus provided our earliest example of "social holiness." He very well could have walked out his ministry all by himself; he certainly was capable. But he didn't. Jesus surrounded himself with community because he knew his disciples and the people of his church would need one another. He faithfully and tirelessly sought out the lonely, the lost, the stranger, and the marginalized. He broke bread with sinners, tax collectors, and even self-righteous Pharisees. Inclusion into his community—the kingdom of heaven—was so important to Jesus that, at the end of the last Passover meal he shared with his disciples, he gave them a new commandment: "Love one another. As I have loved you, so you must love one another. By this everyone will know that you are my disciples, if you love one another" (John 13:34-35).

This commandment soundly resonated with John Wesley. Shortly before his Aldersgate conversion, Wesley experienced a Love Feast with the Moravians in Savannah, Georgia. During Love Feasts (also known as Agape Meals), Christians gather and offer testimonies, prayers, and Scripture passages over a shared meal of bread and water.

Partaken in unity and love, these feasts express the *koinonia* (community, sharing, fellowship) enjoyed by the family of Christ, as alluded to in the Acts of the Apostles (2:42).

Indeed, it was Count Zinzendorf and the Moravians in Germany who, in the early eighteenth century, reintroduced the Love Feast as a service of sharing food, prayer, religious conversation, and hymns. Wesley appreciated the practice: "After evening prayers, we joined with the Germans in one of their love–feasts. It was begun and ended with thanksgiving and prayer, and celebrated in so decent and solemn a manner as a Christian of the apostolic age would have allowed to be worthy of Christ." Eventually, Love Feasts became a regular observance among Methodists around the world.[4]

For a number of years now, many Moravian congregations have served a sweetened bun and cup of coffee for their Love Feasts. Prayer is followed by the singing of hymns, listening to music, and holy conversation with one another about their spiritual walk with God. They observe them on special occasions, such as Watch Night, Good Friday, and Christmas (which may entail additional flourishes). Sometimes Love Feasts are part of the celebration of dates significant to the congregation, such as the anniversary of the church's founding.[5]

Although I have never attended a Moravian Love Feast, I like the idea. A lot. And it brings me right back to that fellowship hall at my grandparents' church. Perhaps what they were doing was just like a Love Feast, with tables of delicious food instead of a sweet bun and coffee. People coming together in unity and love and living out the gospel of Jesus Christ. Caring for one another, welcoming those new to the community, reaching out to those in need, and encouraging one another in faith. That sounds a lot like Jesus's commandment to "Love one another as I have loved you."

The season of Advent is the perfect opportunity to carry out this commandment of Jesus by making room for others at our community tables. Because it really isn't "our" community. It belongs to our Lord and Savior Jesus Christ, who was clear in his mission to include *everyone* at his kingdom table.

"A meal in the presence of God is the goal of salvation," says Tim Chester.[6] The fruit of every tree in the garden of Eden, with the exception of one, was provided by God for Adam and Eve. In celebration of their salvation by the giving of the law—the Mosaic covenant—Moses instructed the Israelites to prepare a burnt offering, and then he and the elders went up and saw God and ate and drank (Exodus 24:5, 9-11). Isaiah foretold of a millennial feast prepared by God for believers on Mount Zion:

> On this mountain the Lord Almighty will prepare
> > a feast of rich food for all peoples,
> a banquet of aged wine—
> > the best of meats and the finest of wines. (25:6)

In Matthew 14:13-21, Jesus fed five thousand people with only five loaves and two fish, and the Last Supper foreshadows the everlasting feast that believers will celebrate with God in the kingdom of heaven (Matthew 26:29).

And in Revelation, we are promised a glorious marriage feast:

Then I heard what sounded like a great multitude, like
the roar of rushing waters and like loud peals of thunder,
shouting:

> *"Hallelujah!*
>   *For our Lord God Almighty reigns.*
> *Let us rejoice and be glad*
>   *and give him glory!*
> *For the wedding of the Lamb has come,*
>   *and his bride has made herself ready.*
> *Fine linen, bright and clean,*
>   *was given her to wear."*

(Fine linen stands for the righteous acts of God's holy people.)

Then the angel said to me, "Write this: Blessed are those
who are invited to the wedding supper of the Lamb!" And he
added, "These are the true words of God." (19:6-9)

"Every time we eat together as Christians we are anticipating this hope," Chester says.[7] And shouldn't we want this gift of hope to be extended not just to our friends and families but to *everyone*? To the strangers in our midst, the lonely, the shut-ins, and those marginalized by our society?

Our society has slowly drifted away from the practice of the love and inclusion that Jesus modeled. Isolation and division seem to be the rule rather than the exception. It is up to us, as God's people, to turn this situation around. I know this is of great concern in heaven.

Do you want to know how I know? Because one night, I had a dream.

1

BE A NEIGHBOR

"Love your neighbor as yourself."
(Mark 12:31)

I awakened from a dead sleep. My wife and I had just returned from a quick trip to northern India. We had not traveled there for tourism but for the dedication of a new school library, which our church had funded. It was a brutal trip. After spending twenty-one hours in the air and struggling to adjust to the twelve-and-a-half-hour time difference, my wife, Bev, and I were worn out. Our bodies were out of sync. Our normal rhythms of sleeping and eating were greatly off-kilter.

But thoughts of the trip, surprisingly, were not what roused me from my slumber. It was a dream!

One might reasonably expect that I had been dreaming about cows. After all, they are everywhere in India because cows are considered sacred in that predominantly Hindu country. You find them standing on busy roads, blocking traffic, or wandering in and out of shops. And it is quite a strange experience for a Westerner!

Or one might expect my dream to be filled with monkeys, for they are ubiquitous; there are even temples dedicated to them.

However, none of these exotic scenes were on my mind. Nor had they been in my dreams. I awakened with one inescapable thought: be a neighbor.

I took it as a word from God. Or perhaps better stated, an *admonishment* from the Lord, for like so many other busy Americans, Bev and I are lousy neighbors. It's shameful, really. For almost twenty years we've lived in the same house, on the same street, in the same eight-home cul-de-sac. Yet, we know hardly any of our neighbors by name.

It's a common problem, I suppose. We say hello occasionally when we run into each other at the cluster of mailboxes. And we always wave while passing in our cars. But seldom do we speak or engage in actual conversation. It's not that we are unfriendly; we are just busy, caught up in our own schedules, our own responsibilities, our own lives.

Sadly, this is the story of too many of us. So, when I woke up that morning with the words "be a neighbor" burning in my mind, I wondered if that message might apply not just to me but to others as well. Perhaps my own experience is a reflection of the wider American culture, which has forgotten the joy of living in community.

Once upon a time neighbors actually knew each other. They were connected. Where I grew up in West Texas, neighbors would form a bond as they sat outside on their wide front porches, constructed to provide relief from the heat of summer. Nowadays, air conditioning makes our living rooms comfortable and our front porches merely decorative.

The advance of technology also has contributed to our isolation. Even developments like garage-door openers and televisions cause us to become more withdrawn into our own homes. Instead of walking up the pathway to our front doors and stopping for a brief chat with neighbors, we pull into our driveways, punch our remote-control devices, drive straight into our garages, and walk directly into our homes without even a chance of saying hello to someone.

Advances in technology affect the ways we entertain ourselves as well. Instead of gathering to play cards or dominoes with neighbors and friends, as once was common, we remain behind closed doors, glued to our television screens. Movie theaters have felt this trend toward isolation, too, as more people choose to stay home and stream their favorite films. Not that "going to the movies" ever equated to real community. Nonetheless, it was a shared experience.

Then came the internet, further disrupting our reliance on one another. In the old days one neighbor might borrow from another neighbor with hardly a thought. With a rap on the door Sue might say, "Hi, Sally. I wonder if you might lend me a cup of sugar?" Sally would gladly agree. And this small exchange would sometimes lead to deeper conversations.

Nowadays, we don't need to go next door to ask for sugar. At the touch of a button on our computer keyboard, we can order it and have it delivered to our front door.

Television, the internet, smartphones: all these technological advances provide substitute relationship opportunities, decreasing our need to connect in person. These modern miracles of communication have drawn even our nuclear families apart. Kids find entertainment in their own rooms, apart from others in the family. And parents often sit in the same room lost in their separate internet worlds. These devices that we say connect us seem to be doing the opposite.

"Americans are richer, more informed and [more] 'connected' than ever—and unhappier, more isolated and less fulfilled."[1] So observes Senator Ben Sasse of Nebraska. "'There is a growing consensus' that loneliness—not obesity, cancer or heart disease—is the nation's 'number one health crisis.'" He further says that "'persistent loneliness' reduces average longevity more than twice as much as does heavy drinking and more than three times as much as obesity, which often is a consequence of loneliness." He points to research that suggests that loneliness is as dangerous to physical health as smoking fifteen cigarettes a day[2] and can exacerbate cognitive decline, such as that caused by Alzheimer's disease. "We're literally dying of despair," Sasse says, of the failure "to fill the hole millions of Americans feel in their lives."[3]

So where does the church fit into this decline in community? After all, we are called to extend Christian hospitality by what Jesus called the second greatest commandment: "Love your neighbor." But are we doing that well? Or have we forgotten, along with so much of Western society, how to love our neighbors?

Acclaimed Christian author C. S. Lewis writes: "Next to the Blessed Sacrament itself, your neighbour is the holiest object presented to your senses"[4] and "Do not waste time bothering whether you 'love' your neighbor; act as if you did. As soon as we do this we find one of the great secrets. When you are behaving as if you loved someone, you will presently come to love him."[5]

Lewis presents an important point for us to consider. First, we must act. Just as God reached out to us in love and grace through Jesus Christ while we were yet sinners, we are to reach out to our neighbors while they are strangers and not yet friends. As the prophet Isaiah says, "Do not hold back" (54:2). Wise words for those of us who might hesitate to invite a stranger—even the stranger next door—into our lives. However, we are called to act. We are called to open the front door.

More than two thousand years ago, a weary young couple desperately knocked on doors of a tiny, bustling community named Bethlehem. Mary and Joseph had arrived there at what turned out to be a terribly inconvenient time. They had to travel from Nazareth to Bethlehem, a hundred-mile trip, perhaps on the back of a donkey, and Mary was expecting her first child. Under these circumstances, most of us would not want to make the journey. But Caesar Augustus had decreed that "a census should be taken of the entire Roman world.... And everyone went to their own town to register" (Mark 2:1, 3).

Surely by the time Joseph and Mary reached Bethlehem, they must have felt worn out. After all, the journey would not have been simple under any circumstances. No automobiles or trains or modern-day roads, of course. No fast-food restaurants along the way; and certainly, no Holiday Inn or Motel 6 with a reservation waiting. Each night was full of adventure and worry. A camp to be made, a fire to be built and lighted without the aid of matches, and the threat of robbers and thieves lurking in the distance, just waiting for a chance to move in and steal their meager belongings.

What time of day or night Joseph and Mary arrived in Bethlehem, we don't know. But we can be sure they were exhausted. Surrounded by other pilgrims in town for the census, the city over capacity, and no reservation in hand, Joseph and Mary must have felt hopeless. Thank goodness someone took them in. We don't know who that was; most often we label that person as a "him" and as an "innkeeper."

Interestingly, no innkeeper is mentioned in Scripture. We infer that one exists because many times when we've heard the Christmas story, we are told that "there was no room in the inn" for Mary and Joseph. Naturally, if there is an inn, we presume there must be an innkeeper. So an innkeeper has become a prominent part of how we tell the Christmas story. And from this telling of the story, we have defined the various characters clearly in our minds. We picture King Herod as the villain—and of course he was, for he was attempting to murder baby Jesus. We see the magi as heroes, traveling a far distance to worship this newborn king. We certainly view the shepherds favorably. After all, the angels beckoned them to the manger. But the imagined innkeeper is typically cast in a negative light, as though he were a grumpy, stonyhearted capitalist who turned his back on the Holy Family in their moment of crisis. In Christmas pageants at churches around the country, a person playing the innkeeper angrily mutters, "There is no room in the inn!"

During this season of the year, carols will fill our sanctuaries. Even some retail stores still play traditional Christmas music. Mary, Joseph, and baby Jesus are the focus of most of the songs, of course. But the shepherds and angels are not far behind. Numerous carols speak of them: "While Shepherds Watched Their Flocks," "It Came upon the Midnight Clear," "Angels We Have Heard on High"—the list is long. The magi are not forgotten; they are recalled in "We Three Kings" and other carols. Even the star and animals are celebrated in some Christmas songs. But who sings about the innkeeper?

Brett Blair observed, "We envision him as a crotchety old man with a nightcap on his head, sticking his head out a second-story window and tersely shouting, 'Take the stable and leave me alone.'"[6]

I wonder if this is a fair depiction. Was the innkeeper truly insensitive, not willing to be bothered by the problems of others? Or was he—assuming it was a he—doing the best he could to provide accommodations in a nearly impossible situation? Interestingly, not all translations of the Bible speak of an inn. In the *Complete Jewish Bible* translation of Luke 2:7 we read, "And she gave birth to her first child, a son. She wrapped him in cloth and laid him down in a feeding trough, because there was no space for them in the living-quarters." *No space for them in the living-quarters.* This provides us an intriguing insight into what may have transpired when Mary and Joseph arrived in Bethlehem.

According to the *Jewish New Testament Commentary*,

> A small, poor village like Bethlehem would not have had an inn. Rather, in most homes, the animals were kept downstairs, while the upper part of the house consisted of a work-room where the

children slept, a separate bedroom for the parents, and a guest room (the last two only if the owner was rich enough to afford them). In a pinch, the space for animals underneath the living quarters would have afforded guests some privacy.[7]

We can speculate that this animal space under the living quarters may have been a basement-like cave, carved out of the rock foundation of the house. It would have provided the livestock protection from the elements. Perhaps a kindhearted homeowner whose home was already full to the brim with guests took pity on this poor, exhausted couple and offered the only place left: the stable under the house. Perhaps it was the homeowner's wife who saw Mary and understood that she was near her time.

What actually transpired is not clear. Luke does not provide details. It's left to our imagination. And for whatever reason, many of us have come to believe that there was an innkeeper and that he was not a good guy. Don't we human beings love to find someone to scorn? We enjoy booing the villain and cheering the hero. Certainly, we carry on that tradition today in our sporting events. So in the popular imagination this supposed innkeeper of Bethlehem became a scoundrel, worthy of our boos and judgment.

Perhaps it is time to consider the innkeeper in a different light. Rather than depicting this person as one who turned away a poor, desperate couple, perhaps we should see him or her as someone who took them in, who made room for them. Such an innkeeper would be an example to us of how to be a good neighbor. We can follow the lead of this Bethlehem homeowner by extending love and warmth to the strangers in our communities, beginning in our own neighborhoods, perhaps with the people next door.

In fact, one of the first things we can learn from the story of Jesus's birth is the importance of welcoming people into our homes and lives, even when it is inconvenient or difficult. If our living rooms are messy and the kids are acting up and the dog won't stop barking...all the better. Perfection should never be an impediment to relationship, and frankly it is comforting to realize that no one really has it all together (though our social-media accounts might make it look that way). The simple truth is that we should never underestimate the power of a welcoming smile or an outstretched hand—even if all we have to offer is a warm, quiet place for someone in need or a sense of community to someone feeling alone.

And these days, more and more people are in need of community. According to the US Census Bureau, about 32 million Americans moved in 2018. That equates to about 10 percent of the population.[8] Families move for a variety of reasons: some because of corporate relocations, others to seek better opportunities, still others in search of cheaper housing, or because of family issues or divorce. Tens of thousands move across state lines. Often these families find themselves far from home. In strange places. Unfamiliar surroundings. Away from the comfort of family and friends. Facing Christmas on their own.

Admittedly, from time to time, many of us want to be alone—for some self time, centering, and recharging our batteries. But almost no one chooses to live a lifetime of loneliness. No one wants to feel left out. No one wants to be forgotten—especially not at Christmas. That is when almost everyone wants to feel part of a community.

Bev and I experienced this need in our first years of marriage. We moved from Wilmore, Kentucky, where we both attended Asbury College, to a small town near Dallas, Texas. Bev taught eighth grade. I was a seminarian at Southern Methodist University. Each weekday I commuted into the city. When we moved into the small county-seat town of Waxahachie, we did not know a soul there.

Although I had grown up in West Texas, my hometown was far away from Dallas. For me, Waxahachie was a different world. And for my wife it was even farther from home and family and familiar surroundings. She was from the Buckeye State and, before college, had lived her entire life in Columbus, Ohio.

Waxahachie was a small, close-knit community of less than forty thousand people. Most folks had lived there all their lives. They knew not only one another but also one another's extended families. Frankly, it was the kind of place where it would be easy to feel alone and left out. After all, the friendship groups were already set, and people were not seeking to add more people to their circles.

Thankfully for us, that was not the case. And that's because of The United Methodist Church. We joined and became active members, and the people welcomed us with open arms. Often after the 11 a.m. worship service, a family would invite us to their home for Sunday dinner, usually with extended family. Instead of feeling like strangers, we felt love and warmth. We felt welcomed.

Looking back, I realize how formative that church community was in our lives. After all these years, we still receive Christmas cards from some of the families. Their friendship and support helped us form positive impressions, which have stood the test of time. We had little to offer in return but that did not matter to them. Jesus had touched their lives, and they were eager to share that love.

Another story comes from one of my associate pastors at our church in The Woodlands, Kimberly Constant. She tells about the time she and her husband, Chad, and their four children moved to Portland, Oregon. It's quite a long way from Texas in terms of distance and culture, and they felt like fish out of water. Not to mention, they didn't know a person or have any family within hundreds of miles. But their neighbors, a family who attended the same church as they did, invited them over for Christmas dinner. Kimberly says that although they barely knew these neighbors, she and Chad accepted, assuming that their neighbors didn't have any family in town either. They assumed that their neighbors invited them out of a mutual need for fellowship. When Kimberly, Chad, and their four children arrived for dinner, they found a big extended family crowded into the home. Grandparents, aunts, uncles, and cousins were there, and tables were crammed into every conceivable space. What Kimberly and Chad discovered was that their new neighbors had made room for them not from loneliness but from love. They welcomed the newcomers not just into their home but also into their family.

I wonder if we might use this Advent season to survey our neighborhoods, to embrace the welcoming spirit of the innkeeper and look intentionally for those around us who might be feeling lonely and left out, those who might need to experience the power of a loving invitation. Perhaps we should focus on opening our doors and extending them a warm invitation, making them feel welcome with whatever provisions we have to offer.

I can't think of a better time to open our doors to those around us than Christmas, to invite a neighboring family into our home to share a meal or perhaps simply host a holiday neighborhood party. After all, doesn't following Jesus require more from us than our usual Advent traditions of singing carols and lighting candles? Don't we need to discover the joy of loving others in tangible ways?

Earlier in this chapter I confessed that Bev and I have been second-rate neighbors. But after the dream I had after returning from India, I realized that we had better remedy that situation! So, Bev and I decided to host a holiday open house for the neighborhood. As I mentioned, we hardly knew our neighbors, and of those we did know, it was only with the vaguest idea of which face went with which house.

We made our list, going house by house:

- Those people who live on the corner and drive the black minivan. I think they have two kids. Check.
- The neighbors across the street who have that cute Goldendoodle named Teddy. (What does that say about us that we know the names of some of our neighbors' dogs but cannot remember the names of the people who own them?) Check.

- Oh, and the Vietnamese couple who walk their baby in a stroller. He's some kind of petroleum engineer, isn't he? Check.

- And did we note the family who live at the end of the cul-de-sac? You know, they're from somewhere in the Middle East, I think. Check.

Sad to say, our level of knowledge of our neighbors resembled that of Ward Cleaver in that classic television sitcom *Leave It to Beaver*. In one episode, the Cleaver family had the opportunity to learn about their new neighbors. Ward, the father, stepped out one day to retrieve the newspaper and was met at the door by his wife, June, as he returned. "I see you contrived to meet our new neighbors," she observed.

"Contrived?" Ward said as he sat down and opened the newspaper. "Why, I just happened to run into him when I went out to get the paper."

June sat directly across from him, her face expectant. "Well?" she queried, wanting to know what he had learned about them.

"Well," Ward answered thoughtfully, "his name's Dawson, and I think he's a broker." He paused. Sensing June's disappointment, he said, "You know, it takes a while to get to know your new neighbors," and returned to reading.

June gave Ward a patient, if not exasperated, look. "Dear, their name is Donaldson. He's with a thermal products company, the assistant sales manager. They put in an application at Briar Cliff, they came here from Binghamton, her mother was a friend of the Bronsons, and she plays bridge."

Ward slowly lowered the paper into his lap while she spoke. "Where'd you get all those details?"

"Oh, I didn't get the *details* yet!" she exclaimed.[9]

Unfortunately, Bev and I resembled Ward more than June. We knew very little about the people who lived around us, even those who lived immediately next door. We were polite but not engaged. We decided to change that, to take a page from June's playbook and take delight in getting to know those who cross our paths. As we made our plans for the Christmas party, we found ourselves truly looking forward to getting to know these people, our neighbors. But just before we purchased the invitations, we discovered that our work, travel, and church schedules were so full that we could not find an open date to host the party!

Not to be deterred and not to disappoint God (I had not forgotten God's middle-of-the-night admonition), we came up with plan B. Bev went shopping and came home with beautifully wrapped loaves of Christmas breads. Over the course of several days, whenever we had a few moments to spare, we went door-to-door in our neighborhood and hand delivered these gifts to everyone on our guest list. Suddenly, the invisible strangers in our neighborhood became people with names. People we determined to know better.

When the next year's Advent season arrived, we were more prepared. We had made certain to reserve a night to host a party. The turnout surprised us. We discovered that others were as eager for some neighborhood connectedness as we were. It was such an enjoyable evening that everyone agreed it should become an annual tradition. Those words of C. S. Lewis certainly rang true for us that year. In reaching out to our neighbors in love, we came to truly love our neighbors.

The truth of the matter is that we need one another. But due to our society's emphasis on self-sufficiency, we too often forget that. It seems that this mutual dependence was understood by the Europeans when they began settling in North America. People recognized that they needed one another, and that need became the glue that held communities together. The settlers did not enjoy the infrastructure that we take for granted today. So they came together, helping one another with home building and barn raisings, and celebrated while doing so.

Today, we tend to presume we don't need our neighbors—until we discover that we do. I remember when I first learned that lesson. It was in the early 1980s. Bev had gone on an overnight retreat with some other women from church. When she informed me of her plans, I was terrified! Me? Alone with two toddlers overnight and most of the day Saturday! Well, I did better soloing than I feared. All seemed fine until the next morning, a Saturday. I was at my desk working on my sermon when the telephone rang. The voice on the other end of the line said with alarm, "Pastor, you haven't forgotten our wedding, have you?"

Immediately, I responded, "Oh, my goodness...um, no...well, yes! Please remind me of the time of the wedding." The bride replied, "It's supposed to begin now: 10 a.m.!" Embarrassed, I admitted I hadn't yet showered or shaved, and it would take me a little bit to get there.

She was remarkably calm, and said, "OK, not to worry. We will rearrange the order of things. We can have the champagne reception first while we wait for you to arrive." What I did not tell the bride was that I had two toddlers at home that I had to deal with first. Panic set in: I had no idea where to turn for babysitting help. That's when I decided I would just go next door and ask the neighbor to watch them. Honestly, I barely knew these people, but I did know through my wife that they attended a small charismatic church nearby. I boldly knocked on the door and explained my situation. To my relief, this neighbor said she would be happy to keep the children, and off I raced to the wedding.

Yes, we do need one another. I've been moved to tears by the beauty of neighbors who come together in the aftermath of a natural disaster. In the Houston area, we have been hit by several massive storms in recent years. In the days and weeks following these events, neighbors and complete strangers helped one another remove debris, muck out flooded homes, cut up fallen trees, and hold giant neighborhood barbecues to use up food that would otherwise spoil from lack of refrigeration.

The act of being a good neighbor can take on many forms. Planning a party, inviting someone over for a meal or a cup of coffee, or simply hand delivering a special treat can get the ball rolling. Being a good neighbor can look like extending a hand in the aftermath of a storm or lending an ear to someone who longs to be heard.

My friend Jennifer Morgan tells a moving story about how her three dogs literally broke down a barrier in her neighborhood, beginning with her fence.

When they first moved into their house, she and her husband did not take the time to get to know the neighbors. Like Bev and me, they politely waved to each other as they were coming and going. But Jenn's three whippets and two neighbor dogs began to engage in exuberant barking "conversations" on a regular basis. Often these barking matches would escalate, and the dogs would lean into the fence, eager to crash through to the other side. The result was frequently broken fence slats.

With each broken slat, Jenn and her husband, Guy, slowly got to know their neighbors, through exchanging names and phone numbers, contributing to a joint lumber fund for replacement slats, and exchanging ideas to outwit their persistent pups. Then late one afternoon, Jenn's doorbell rang.

It was her neighbor, with another broken fence report. As he was about to leave, he stopped, paused for a minute, and then said, "I know you are a woman of faith. My wife and I see you and your husband going to church on Sunday mornings. Would you mind praying for my daughter?"

The neighbor's eyes filled with tears as he told Jenn that his daughter, a relatively young woman, had recently been diagnosed with cancer. After listening to his story, Jenn proceeded to ask if they could pray together right then and there, on her front porch. And they did, hand in hand, oblivious to the traffic driving by and a lawn mower blaring across the street. In that moment, what had first been small acts of reaching out (mostly because of the actions of their dogs) became true neighborly bonding. Sometimes we forget the power of a listening ear, of simply making ourselves available.

Noted author Edgar Guest came into his prime around the time of World War I. One of his books, *A Heap o' Livin'*, became a best seller and earned him a significant sum of money. But Guest is best known and loved for his poetry.

When Guest and his wife were a young couple starting their family, they moved to a new city. For them, it was a large and strange city, and they struggled to adjust. Then their child became ill. Try as they might, try as the doctor might, their child could not be saved. It was a terrible loss for them. They felt the weight of the world on their shoulders.

The morning after their child died, this man with a poet's spirit and heart went to the corner drugstore. The druggist motioned for him to come behind the counter "where he put both his kindly hands upon my shoulders and said, 'Eddie, I can't tell you what is in my heart. I am sorry—sorry! I just wanted to say that if—if you need money, come to me.'"

And that's all he could say; the only words he could find.

Guest reminisced upon that incident. He said, "Jim Potter [the druggist] may have forgotten the incident, but I shall never forget it. To me it stands out vividly; the blossoming of a neighbor into a true friend."[10]

A professor I have known and admired for many years is Dr. William Abraham. He teaches at Perkins School of Theology at Southern Methodist University. With a full white beard, he looks like an Old Testament prophet, but it is his Irish accent that is most quickly noticed. At the age of sixteen he converted to Christianity.

God used a Methodist preacher as the catalyst. Dr. Abraham now says "that preacher did the hardest thing for any preacher to do: he kept his mouth shut for thirty minutes and listened as a mixed-up boy poured out his frustrations, hurts, and questions." He explains, "God hooked me through the patient listening of that godly man."[11]

Perhaps the best gift of hospitality we can give this Advent is to make room in our busy schedules for the person who simply needs to be heard, to know someone cares. Throughout Scripture we are encouraged to open our homes and our hearts to others, to make ourselves available.

But with this encouragement also comes a warning. We must take care that making room doesn't become a chore, just one more item to check off our Christmas to-do list, but is something that comes from a heart overflowing with God's grace. In his Letter to the Romans the apostle Paul writes, "Share with the Lord's people who are in need. Practice hospitality" (12:13). Did you catch that? Paul is calling us to a continual attitude and practice. We should *always* exhibit a welcoming spirit and look for ways to share God's love.

And in 1 Peter 4:8-9 we read, "Above all, love each other deeply, because love covers over a multitude of sins. Offer hospitality to one another without grumbling." Without complaining! That means we are to be the kind of people who reach out with a smile on our face! We are to appreciate our holiday company as blessings rather than intruders. Ouch! That feels personal because, I confess, I've not always had this attitude.

Let's face it, often our expectations during the holidays exceed reality. We want everything to be perfect. We think the holiday is supposed to be joyous. Without even knowing it, we can confuse hospitality with entertaining: a recipe for stress and exhaustion. Why? Entertaining often makes us perpetuate the myth that we are perfect. We can feel the pressure to put up a facade that says, "My life is wonderful; my children never, ever get in trouble or make a mess; and no one ever says something inappropriate when company is in the house."

Hospitality, on the other hand, doesn't worry about perfection. Instead, when we practice hospitality, we recognize that we are all a mess in some way or another. Wouldn't it be more fun just to relax and enjoy one another's company? And there's something else to consider, an even deeper meaning of the word *hospitality*. This word comes from the same source as two similar sounding words: *hospice*, which means shelter, and *hospital*, which is a place of healing. In this light, hospitality becomes truly more of an attitude than an action; more of a way of interacting with people in our community than a one-time attempt to impress the neighbors. True hospitality involves providing a shelter for others with our words and actions. True hospitality involves healing of lonely hearts, of disconnected lives, and of the fear of being unknown and unloved.

Christmas with family can be challenging because our expectations are elevated. We plan perfection into every aspect of a family gathering. Yet often we find ourselves falling back into old, unhealthy patterns from earlier years. In our families, we lapse into already established roles that seem to dictate who we are and how we are to act (based on gender, birth order, and family rules and rituals).[12]

In one family I know, a grown sister is always on the outs with some other family member. She has been this way seemingly since birth. Often she holds a grudge against a sibling from the previous holiday over some perceived slight or an argument over silly matters. As a result, none of her siblings want her around. But she is single, has few friends, and is lonely. For this family every holiday is a time when extra grace is required.

I imagine this strikes a chord with a lot of people. Many of us probably have at least one "toxic relative," a person who can be especially challenging, irritating, or socially awkward. Often these are the people who most need love and affirmation, but they can be so difficult. And during the holidays, especially Christmas, there is an expectation by many—barring intolerable situations such as abuse and violence—that we should come together as families, which often pressures us to put up with someone we would generally avoid. No, it is not always easy or convenient to welcome certain people, even some family members, into our homes. But this is exactly what love commands us to do. God certainly reminded me of that in the dream I described at the beginning of this chapter. All of us need to connect with someone who cares. Perhaps this was the first gift presented to Mary and Joseph on that bustling starry night in Bethlehem, before the wise men arrived with frankincense, gold, and myrrh. Perhaps it was the gift of an innkeeper who cared. Someone with a listening ear who heard their need; someone who, though the inn was filled, made room. A gift like that was probably more valuable to Mary and Joseph than precious spices and gold.

Throughout the busyness and bustle and challenges that each Advent season brings, may we remember to embrace the welcoming spirit of the innkeeper by opening our homes and hearts to one another. For in doing so, we discover the true meaning of the season.

2

WELCOME STRANGERS

He defends the cause of the fatherless and the widow, and loves the foreigner residing among you, giving them food and clothing. And you are to love those who are foreigners, for you yourselves were foreigners in Egypt.
(Deuteronomy 10:18-19)

When our church was in its infancy, back in the late 1970s, I tried to visit every mother when her child was born. Since our new congregation was small, that wasn't difficult. Most of the births occurred in the same community hospital, which was only about fourteen miles away. However, unlike today, when family and friends are welcomed into patients' rooms, hospitals back then were not visitor friendly. There were set visiting hours, and only two were allowed in a room at the same time. Nonetheless, I made certain to see each new member of our church family and offer prayer.

I miss those days when mothers typically stayed in the hospital for four or five nights after giving birth. That allowed time for me to find out about the birth and get to the hospital before the mother was released. Once the young family is back home, a pastoral visit—any visit—can feel like more of an intrusion. The parents wonder, *Is the house clean? Will the other children behave?*

These days, most mothers remain only one to two nights, so the window of catching the young family at the hospital is short. Another challenge for me these days is the sheer number of babies born into our church each year. Now we typically have more than two hundred births annually.

Each Advent I think about depictions of that holy night and how it seemed like a crowd of strangers barged into Mary and Joseph's "birthing room." Not everyone was there yet, in spite of common representations of the manger scene. I am familiar with manger scenes! My wife, Bev, enjoys collecting them. There's no telling how many we have stored in the attic; dozens, I suspect. Certainly, we own more than we can display any given year. These crèches come in many styles and from many places. Some are from Bethlehem and are beautifully carved from olive wood. Others we purchased on mission trips to South America and Africa. Still others come from Christmas markets in Europe. Some of those are exquisitely painted porcelain; others are made of felt, designed for children to pick up and handle. They come in many different styles, all with the same purpose: to remind us of the events surrounding Jesus's birth.

Regardless of their style or country of origin, most nativity scenes have one thing in common: everyone is there. All the characters are assembled: angels, shepherds, magi, sheep, cows, often camels and donkeys, and of course, baby Jesus and his parents.

We conveniently compress the Christmas story. The wise men

did not arrive until sometime later, of course, but somehow the crèche appears better if we put them into the scene as well.

Can you imagine how crowded that first night must have been, even without the wise men? We don't know exactly when the wise men arrived nor where they came from, except from the East.

That's what Matthew's Gospel says: "After Jesus was born in Bethlehem in Judea, during the time of King Herod, Magi from the east came to Jerusalem and asked, 'Where is the one who has been born king of the Jews? We saw his star when it rose and have come to worship him'" (2:1-2).

Who were these magi? Most Bible scholars speculate that they were likely Persians. Bethlehem's Church of the Nativity, commissioned by the Roman Emperor Constantine around AD 330, is traditionally believed to stand over Jesus's birthplace. The church survived the Persian invasion in 614. Legend has it that the commander Shahrbaraz was stirred by the portrayal above the church entrance of the three magi, depicted in the garb of Persian Zoroastrian priests; thus he ordered that the building remain intact.[1]

Just how far the wise men traveled, how long it took, and how many there were are unknown. Traditionally, we have assumed three because of their three gifts. These holy men are thought to have been skilled in philosophy and astronomy. They studied the heavens. They arrived saying, "We saw his star when it rose and have come to worship him" (Matthew 2:2).

Their coming brought trouble (we will get to that), but let's not forget their immediate impact. They came bearing gifts. They came to worship. They came to discover this newborn king. We know all that, right? But Joseph and Mary *didn't* know this! They did not know the nature of the wise men's intentions; at least not when they first arrived. All Mary and Joseph knew was that more strangers were at their door, asking to come in.

Don't you suspect Mary and Joseph were already worn out from company? First there were the smelly shepherds. At least they were human beings. It was those angels who really freaked them out, wouldn't you guess? And they were singing. All Mary wanted was some quiet. Some rest. A good night's sleep.

Think of it: she had just given birth and already she was entertaining guests! But here's what is noteworthy: she did it. Mary and Joseph welcomed them all in: the angels, the shepherds, the innkeeper, I suppose. And in the days or months ahead when life seemed to be settling down: the wise men showed up.

Can you imagine the conversation? It might have gone like this:

"Honey, guests have arrived!" Joseph might have said.

"Surely not! More company, more entertaining," Mary might have responded.

Who could blame these young parents if they felt overwhelmed? More strangers barging into their "maternity suite." And these guests must have been challenging. They wore strange clothes, had unfamiliar accents, and arrived on smelly animals, which were now grazing in their front yard.

Try to find yourself a new mother who would jump at the chance to welcome a group of men who were dirty from a long journey and allow those same men to get anywhere near her baby! You will be hard-pressed. Most new moms have a checklist of conditions one must meet even to be allowed into the same room as their precious baby: Are you sick? Have you been near anyone who has been sick? Did you wash your hands? And please use hand sanitizer. Oh, and do you mind wearing a face mask?

I'm exaggerating, but you get the idea. To Mary it must have seemed as though all these unexpected guests would never stop coming. And remember, Mary and Joseph were not even in their own house! They were still living in borrowed quarters.

Yet once more this young couple provides us with a lesson in gracious hospitality. They invited these wise men—strangers, really—into their lodging and allowed them to worship their son. During a time in life when most people want to close their doors and draw an invisible line of protection around their new family and their vulnerable infant, Mary and Joseph opened theirs. That is another Christmas miracle!

Mary and Joseph discovered that showing hospitality brought blessings to their lives. The magi, for instance, came bearing gifts: gold, frankincense, and myrrh. More important, their guests brought love and encouragement, helping this young couple realize even more fully just what kind of special child Jesus was. These unexpected guests—angels, shepherds, and wise men—all came for the same reason: to worship this newborn king.

Hospitality is always a two-way street. Yes, it takes effort to welcome people into our homes, and the guests appreciate the hospitality.

But we benefit too. In fact, I will go so far as to say we benefit most when we are the hosts. There is something about entertaining that brings its own reward.

The Bible says in Hebrews, "Keep on loving one another as brothers and sisters. Do not forget to show hospitality to strangers, for by so doing some people have shown hospitality to angels without knowing it" (13:1-2).

Welcoming friends is one thing. Opening our doors to strangers is another matter, right? But it can also be rewarding. It provides us the opportunity to get to know new people and to learn about their lives. It widens our circle of friends.

Because my church is located in a fast-growing area with a large number of corporate transfers, we are intentional about helping new people connect with others. Leaving assimilation to chance can be hit or miss—more often *miss*. We decided to provide opportunities for people to develop friendships. Each year we encourage people to register for a ministry we call Dinner for Eight. People submit their names and are assigned to a random group from the church. All we ask is for the group to come together, either in a home or restaurant, four times during the year. Sometimes when talking with parishioners who are friends, I will ask them how they got acquainted. More than once, the answer has been, "Oh, we met at a Dinner for Eight some years ago and really clicked. We've been good friends ever since." This is an easy way for strangers to meet new people and become friends.

Another effective program we offer, New Roots, welcomes women who are new to the area or are going through a major life change. This program provides the opportunity to grow new friendships as well as learn about the community and the resources available to them. Both of these ministries help alleviate the inevitable stress and loneliness of those who are in a new place or situation.

Being a stranger can carry with it a certain stigma. In our culture, as well as many others, we have been conditioned to avoid strangers. What we don't know about another person seems to threaten our own well-being. Strangers are scary; at least that is the way most of us were reared and what we have taught our own children. Though we might not use that exact phrase, we do tell our children not to talk to strangers. A song written to teach children about these risks warns, "Don't go with strangers, they are not your friends. / This is a rule that only parents can bend."[2]

Sadly, we live in a time when caution is necessary, especially for children. But I wonder if we have carried this fear into adulthood and have senselessly hindered opportunities to get to know some really good people. Jesus understood this; no one was truly a stranger to him. Meeting a stranger was an opportunity to demonstrate love and inclusion into the community of God.

For every bad encounter, surely there are hundreds of good ones, when strangers come to our assistance showing love and concern. Recently I read about a young woman who received a call while grocery shopping, informing her that her grandfather had died. The death wasn't unexpected, but to hear the news was still a shock.

> I just stood there and went white and numb. An
> older couple happened to be standing near me and

sensed something was wrong. They asked but I couldn't make words come out. They sat with me for a while, got ahold of my best friend to come pick me up, AND bought the groceries in my cart.... That was one of the worst days of my life and I miss my grandpa every single day, but that kindness and humanity makes me cry in a good way.[3]

I had a similar experience of receiving kindness from a total stranger. Last summer, my wife and I visited Florence, Italy, with our granddaughter. The first evening, we walked to a restaurant that we had carefully selected by reading online reviews. While reading the menu and relishing the thought of each dish, I suddenly realized my wallet was missing. "Oh, my goodness," I exclaimed. "I've been pickpocketed on the way here!" My granddaughter calmly said, "Papa, you probably left your wallet on the bed in your room. I remember seeing it there."

Embarrassed, we excused ourselves and raced back to the hotel, retracing our route. At every corner, I suspiciously looked around, staring at the bystanders. *Whoever did it is probably still around at one of these intersections*, I thought. I imagined catching the crook fleecing some other innocent tourist, nabbing him, and getting my own wallet back. Of course, that did not happen.

Back at the hotel, my wallet was not on the bed. Now I was truly downcast. Dejected, we returned to the restaurant and started again. Partway into dinner I felt my cell phone vibrating and checked my e-mail out of habit. To my astonishment it was a message from a storekeeper who had found my missing wallet, took the trouble of looking for contact information, found a business card with our church's phone number, and called. My assistant gave the shopkeeper my e-mail address, and the shopkeeper notified me. I was dumbfounded. When we searched the internet to find the shop's location, we discovered that it was only a three-minute walk from where we were dining.

That evening I learned a valuable lesson. Strangers are more likely to be kind persons who will go out of their way to help than they are to be malevolent thieves waiting to pounce. Interesting how we often presume danger from strangers and how that attitude shapes the way we relate to them.

First John 4:7 tells us to "love one another, for love comes from God. Everyone who loves has been born of God and knows God." Developing true fellowship with other believers is important, but our call to welcome others extends beyond the church house. We are surrounded by strangers every day, including those who are new to our area and those who are isolated due to age, senior-care housing, and health issues. The effect is the same: loneliness; missing the comfort of family and friends; facing Christmas, and every other day, alone. As followers of Jesus, it is our responsibility, and hopefully, our delight, to offer love and inclusion to these members of our communities who need it the most. And it can begin with paying attention to those living in our own neighborhoods.

One member in our church wrote me about how she met Gladys, an elderly woman who had moved into her neighborhood.

"Back then I was a single mother," our member shared in her letter. "Every morning was a struggle just to get my two kids ready for school and out the door. While I was getting ready for work each day, I would hear Gladys walking out her back door for her morning walk. Why I started doing this I don't know, but when I would hear Gladys walking outside, I would fling open my window and shout, "Good morning, Gladys. I hope you have a wonderful day."

This young single mother felt she hardly had time in the day to sneeze, much less notice a neighbor. Still, she made sure to greet Gladys each day. It didn't seem all that consequential or significant in the way of hospitality. But, she wrote, "I came to realize that just saying 'good morning' meant something. And over time that small connection led to a deep bond."

These days Aunt Gladys (as her neighbor now calls her) is ninety-six and living in Florida in a nursing home. But Aunt Gladys still calls her former neighbor frequently to stay in touch. And the old woman always says, "I still remember your voice singing out 'good morning' to me every day. It always brought such comfort to know that someone cared."

What if we used this Advent time to survey our neighborhoods? To look for the "Aunt Gladys" living in our midst? To seek out those around us who might be feeling lonely and left out? To notice those who might be hurting? To look for those who might benefit from just hearing a friendly voice and seeing a warm smile or those who might feel happy to receive a loving invitation? Perhaps we could focus on opening our doors and reaching out to them, making them feel welcome.

My colleague Kimberly Constant told me of a recent conversation she had with a woman named Sue who had just moved into town. Sue and her family have been visiting our church, and over lunch she told Kimberly about the difficulty of adjusting to the move. It was not just a new location; it was a different environment and unfamiliar culture for them.

The woman said, "I am an immigrant. I don't have a Social Security card, which means I can't get a Texas driver's license, which means I can't work. I can't open a bank account. I can't do anything. I feel like I am nobody, like I don't have an identity."

And this is a woman from Canada! She speaks English and shares our faith. She seems like someone who has lived in the United States her entire life. How must immigrants feel when they come from some place that is very different from ours, a place where the language, culture, religion, style of dress, and pastimes are completely different from ours?

Whether it is a lonely elderly person, a young family who moved far from home, or a homesick immigrant from Canada, these are just the kind of people Jesus sought out. He had a gift for finding left-out people and making room for them.

I wonder if Jesus's welcoming attitude and sensitivity toward strangers started with his parents. After all, Joseph and Mary made room for others from the very beginning of Jesus's life. Perhaps hospitality became Jesus's lifelong pattern. Maybe he became accustomed to having guests in his home. I've got a hunch that those early life experiences helped shape his understanding of neighbors and of community.

There's another experience from Jesus's early life that surely made an impact on him. It's when he and his parents were themselves strangers, after escaping to Egypt. They were forced to flee for safety and became refugees far from home, dependent on the kindness of others.

We all remember that the wise men brought gifts of gold, frankincense, and myrrh. We are prone to overlook, however, that they also brought trouble. Matthew says,

> After Jesus was born in Bethlehem in Judea, during the time of King Herod, Magi from the east came to Jerusalem and asked, "Where is the one who has been born king of the Jews? We saw his star when it rose and have come to worship him."
>
> When King Herod heard this he was disturbed, and all Jerusalem with him. When he had called together all the people's chief priests and teachers of the law, he asked them where the Messiah was to be born. "In Bethlehem in Judea," they replied, "for this is what the prophet has written:
>
> "'But you, Bethlehem, in the land of Judah,
> are by no means least among the rulers of Judah;
> for out of you will come a ruler
> who will shepherd my people Israel.'"
>
> Then Herod called the Magi secretly and found out from them the exact time the star had appeared. He sent them to Bethlehem and said, "Go and search carefully for the child. As soon as you find him, report to me, so that I too may go and worship him." (2:1-8)

Herod sent the magi on a secret mission to find Jesus, but he gave them a false reason. He claimed he wanted to worship the child, but he had something more sinister in mind.

Maybe you remember what happened: Warned in a dream, the magi did not go back to Herod. They skipped past Jerusalem and returned home by another way. And when Herod learned that he had been duped, he became furious and gave orders to kill all the male children in Bethlehem and its vicinity who were two years old and younger.

All this might sound far-fetched to our modern ears, as if the Bible writers embellished the story for effect. *Really?* we might think. *What king, especially a powerful ruler like Herod, feels threatened by a child?*

Curious, yes, but history supports Matthew's account. Herod was "insanely suspicious.... If he suspected anyone as a rival to his power, that person was promptly eliminated." Victims of his suspicion included his wife, her mother, and three of his own sons. All of his killing prompted Caesar Augustus to comment "that it was safer to be Herod's pig than Herod's son."[4]

Kill all the children in Bethlehem two years of age and younger? No problem for King Herod. Yes, Herod was troubled, as Matthew records, and all in Jerusalem with him. They knew what was at stake. They knew what this maniacal king was capable of. But Herod's scheme didn't work. Joseph was warned in a dream to take Mary and Jesus and flee to Egypt.

We tend to forget that our Lord himself was once a political refugee. I wonder if there are lessons we can glean from the Holy Family's experience. It is true that they lived during an entirely different time, in a sparsely populated area that had no national boundaries and where people were largely nomadic.

For example, traders, shepherds, and others traveled freely from location to location, to different city-states and kingdoms, "to ply their trades and make a living on the move. Craftsmen would spend periods away from home hiring themselves out."[5]

The Holy Family found themselves fleeing their ancestral home, the land of their birth, by necessity, escaping to a country where people practiced a different religion, spoke a different language, and ate different kinds of food. How strange it must have felt!

Immigration is a hot-button issue these days. As Christians we can and do differ about the right approach to this vexing problem, with some supporting stronger borders and others advocating for a more open approach. It's not easy to discern the best governmental policy, but we cannot allow this national debate to blind us to our mandate as Christians. No matter what our political affiliation may be, when it comes to immigration and border enforcement, one principle on which Christians can agree is that every person is a child of God and is worthy in God's sight. We can agree that our love should know no boundaries. And we can pray for that day when we can live in a world free of conflict. We can pray for a day when neighbors do not feel the need to build fences, either around their own homes or at national borders. But until that time when God's kingdom shall come to earth as it is in heaven, Christians will undoubtedly struggle to find consensus on immigration policies.

While the Scriptures do not prescribe specific immigration policy that should govern nations, God instructs the Israelites on how to treat foreigners in their land.

> *"When a foreigner resides among you in your land, do not mistreat them. The foreigner residing among you must be treated as your native-born. Love them as yourself, for you were foreigners in Egypt. I am the LORD your God."*
> *(Leviticus 19:33-34)*

God's people were commanded to love migrants; after all, as God reminded them, they experienced firsthand what it is like to dwell in a land that was not their own.

> *He defends the cause of the fatherless and the widow, and loves the foreigner residing among you, giving them food and clothing. And you are to love those who are foreigners, for you yourselves were foreigners in Egypt.*
> *(Deuteronomy 10:18-19)*

And what about those immigrants who are already here? How should we treat them? Is it not our Christian duty to provide all possible spiritual care for pilgrims, aliens, exiles, and migrants of every kind? Whether our neighborhood is their haven of safety for a season or for the long term, we are called by Scripture to treat strangers in a strange land with dignity and respect. Getting to know some of these strangers and their stories has a way of softening our hearts. Let me tell you about an example.

Farhat Popal was only three weeks old when her family fled Kabul, Afghanistan. For decades, her parents had lived a wonderful life surrounded by friends and relatives. Her parents told her that it was "filled with Friday picnics, movies with friends, trips to the countryside to visit relatives, and a myriad of everyday things that made life beautiful." But, when the Soviet Union invaded Afghanistan in 1979, Farhat's family knew all of that was coming to an end.

They fled in the 1980s, in the midst of the ten-year war. Tragically, they lost almost everything.

Despite the complexity of the immigration process, the Popal family became American citizens in 2004, twelve years after they moved to the United States. "We were grateful because we felt like we had a place here, as if Americans all over the country had saved us a spot at the table," Farhat explains. "To me, being an American means saving others a spot at the table, those who may be fleeing war and conflict like my family did, poverty and economic marginalization, political or religious persecution, or any other number of reasons why a person or family would migrate from one country to another."[6]

How long did the Holy Family live in Egypt? We don't know. How did they survive? We don't know. Was Joseph able to gain employment as a carpenter? We don't know. Did Mary or Joseph have relatives there? Or was there perhaps a colony of Jews who welcomed them in and helped them survive? Again, we simply don't know. Perhaps it was that gift of gold from the wise men that kept them going for a while. The Gospel writers do not say. But the Bible does reveal that the Holy Family returned to Nazareth while Jesus was still a boy. We know this because of Luke's account of the time twelve-year-old Jesus stayed behind in Jerusalem after his parents had left for home. Once his parents discovered that he was not with them, they searched frantically for him before finding him at the temple (Luke 2:41-50).

Let's allow our imaginations to fill in some blanks for a moment.

I think that Mary and Joseph's pattern of welcoming strangers into their home continued once they were back in Nazareth. Don't you imagine they told stories around the supper table with Jesus and their other children listening, soaking in every word, about the time they escaped for their lives? How they had to flee the fury of King Herod? How they were taken in by strangers and given shelter in Egypt?

Perhaps each year on Jesus's birthday, Mary retold the story about the chaos on the night of his birth. How, thank God, an innkeeper took them in when everybody else had turned them away. And how strangers kept appearing for months on end, just wanting to get a glimpse of the child.

And maybe Mary and Joseph always felt the stress and the importance of welcoming strangers and of caring for those in need. Jesus passed on that lesson to us, didn't he? Remember the parable of the good Samaritan? Luke records a conversation between Jesus and an expert in the law:

> On one occasion an expert in the law stood up to test Jesus. "Teacher," he asked, "what must I do to inherit eternal life?"
>
> "What is written in the Law?" he replied. "How do you read it?"
>
> He answered, "'Love the Lord your God with all your heart and with all your soul and with all your strength and with all your mind'; and, 'Love your neighbor as yourself.'"
>
> "You have answered correctly," Jesus replied. "Do this and you will live."
>
> But he wanted to justify himself, so he asked Jesus, "And who is my neighbor?" (10:25-29)

How did Jesus respond? We read in the verses that follow that he told a story about a traveler heading to Jericho who was mugged, beaten, and left for dead. Both a Jewish priest and a Levite passed by the man, and both crossed the road to avoid him. But then a Samaritan, a stranger to the area from a place the Jewish people despised, stopped to help. When the Samaritan saw the man's condition, his heart went out to him. He bandaged his wounds. Then he lifted him onto his donkey, took him to an inn, and made him comfortable.

In the morning the unnamed Samaritan gave the innkeeper two days' worth of wages and said, "'Look after him. . . . and when I return, I will reimburse you for any extra expense you may have.'

"Which of these three do you think was a neighbor to the man who fell into the hands of robbers?" Jesus asked.

"The one who had mercy on him," the legal expert responded.

Jesus said, "Go and do likewise" (vv. 35-37).

Go and do likewise. That is exactly how the townspeople in Fairplay, Colorado, responded on Thanksgiving weekend in 2019. A fierce snow storm left more than seven hundred people stranded on US Highway 285, and residents became modern-day good Samaritans. "When the emergency shelter in Fairplay ran out of blankets Saturday night, volunteers went door-to-door collecting extras from locals. When the hotels ran out of rooms, managers let stranded travelers sleep in the lobbies. When the shelter's cots were full, volunteers spread out the high school's wrestling mats to try to keep as many people as possible off the floor."[7]

The tiny mountain town of 762 people suddenly doubled in size, but instead of fearing the stranded strangers, the local citizens welcomed them warmly on a cold winter night.

For Jesus, it did not matter who was in need. Everyone matters to God. Everyone has value. And we are instructed to show mercy, kindness, and hospitality to everyone who crosses our path. Being a good neighbor is not a matter of geography but of hospitality. It requires caring for people who look like us, talk like us, and live near us—and those who don't.

Immigration, becoming strangers in a strange land, is never easy. Our Lord experienced this difficulty not only when his family had to flee to Egypt for safety but also when he first came to earth. Isn't the Incarnation the ultimate example of migration? The story of Christmas is rooted in the truth that God's only begotten son left heaven and came to earth—Immanuel, God with us. The apostle John emphasized this truth in the opening of his Gospel when he declares, "The Word became flesh and made his dwelling among us. We have seen his glory, the glory of the one and only Son, who came from the Father, full of grace and truth" (1:14).

That is the very heart of Christmas. We would expect his coming to be welcomed with joy, but as John writes, "He was in the world, and though the world was made through him, the world did not recognize him. He came to that which was his own, but his own did not receive him" (1:10–11).

Professor Octavio Javier Esqueda reminds us that all Christians are immigrants. When we make room in our hearts for Jesus, we become citizens of heaven and now live as foreigners and strangers on earth, as we read in Hebrews 11:13. This understanding should cause us to "have compassion for those foreigners who come from different regions and countries because we recognize that we all are also foreigners and exiles on earth (1 Peter 2:11)." Knowing that our Lord was a refugee should lead us to make room in our hearts and communities for the foreigners and immigrants among us.[8]

Long ago the wise men came seeking the newborn king. They bore gifts of gold and essential oils. They also bore the gift of worship. This Advent season, what gifts, along with our worship, can we offer to Jesus? What about hospitality, which was so central to his life? Why don't we enter Christmas with welcoming hearts? Making room for the strangers in our midst, those whom Jesus loves so dearly, is surely one of the most precious gifts we can offer our Savior—at Christmas and always.

3

LEAVE THE LIGHT ON

The people walking in darkness
have seen a great light;
on those living in the land of deep darkness
a light has dawned.
(Isaiah 9:2)

Of the many treasured memories I have of my childhood, one of the most vivid comes from a family trip to Carlsbad Caverns National Park, located in the Guadalupe Mountains of New Mexico. I was in the seventh grade in Midland, Texas, when my parents decided that we would go see these famous caves.

Carlsbad Caverns is made up of an enormous main cavern and a network of smaller rooms and chambers, numbering more than 119 in all. And they have such intriguing names: King's Palace, Left Hand Tunnel, Lower Cave, Spider Cave, Hall of the White Giant, Papoose Room, Queen's Chamber, Chocolate High...I think my favorite is a tie between Chocolate High and Spider Cave, but Spider Cave probably has the edge. And then there's the Bat Cave, from which thousands of bats fly each night. Altogether a rather spooky place, those caverns.

I clearly recall how eerie it felt to descend so deep below ground to explore the caves. I had never done that before. And I remember how cool it was—fifty-six degrees, year-round—quite a contrast to the blistering desert heat above ground. That trip made quite an impression on me. But what I remember most, above everything, was when the park ranger told us all to sit down once we were deep inside the main cavern. He gave us a brief talk about stalagmites and stalactites. (I still get those two confused!) And then he announced, "I'm turning out the lights. Don't move."

There we sat, deep below the ground, with no light. Pitch black. Nothing. Let me tell you something: you don't know how *dark* dark can be until you are in a cave with no light. Darkness can create expectation and mystery, such as when the lights dim before a play. It can be an inconvenience, such as when the electricity fails after a powerful storm. And darkness also can be deadly.

When we read about darkness in Scripture, it's always an oppressive, despotic, deadly force. You may remember that darkness is mentioned in the very second sentence of the Bible: "In the beginning God created the heavens and the earth. Now the earth was formless and empty, darkness was over the surface of the deep" (Genesis 1:1-2).

Darkness was everywhere. So, what did God do? God brought light. "And God said, 'Let there be light,' and there was light. God saw that the light was good" (Genesis 1:3-4).

God saw that the light was good. This should tell us something about darkness and God. They are opposing forces—enemies, if you will. Good versus evil. We understand this concept well, for it is ingrained in our daily forms of thought and speech. We use *dark* to describe pain or discouragement, such as "the dark night of the soul," "I'm wandering around in the dark," or "I'm in a dark place right now."

Conversely, we speak of light in a positive way; for example, "There's a light at the end of the tunnel" and "I'm beginning to see the light." When God began work on creation, the very first task was to bring light to the darkness.

The presence of light has a profound effect on the forms of darkness we encounter. Deep inside that Carlsbad cave, the dark was thick and foreboding, and I wished the ranger would hurry and turn the lights back on. And that's when he did something completely unexpected. He struck a match. A single match. And he held it aloft. We all gasped as the entire, enormous cavern was suddenly illuminated— you could see everywhere—and the cave was beautiful in the match's flickering light. That mammoth expanse of darkness was no "match" for the light of a single, solitary flame.

As a pastor, I've noticed that there are several seasons and holidays on our liturgical calendar that beautifully speak to the presence of light in our world, such as that original Easter Sunday morning when the first rays of dawn exposed the empty tomb and the resurrection of Jesus. I am always up before dawn on Easter morning, preparing for our many worship services. And I never fail to feel chills of joy as the first rays of light fall upon my backyard, heralding, once again, the good news of our risen Savior. And then there is the miraculous day of Pentecost, when the light of heaven appeared as tongues of fire as the Holy Spirit was delivered to the disciples and humankind.

But I think my favorite day on the liturgical calendar falls during Advent, on Christmas Eve. We gather together with hearts filled with expectation. We wear our festive clothes. We come to sing carols. We come for Holy Communion. We come to sing, at the end of the worship service, "Silent Night." And we come to pass the light—the light that starts with the Christ candle.

Just before we sing that final hymn, the chandeliers and spotlights are all turned off and the sanctuary becomes dark. We begin to sing. "Silent night, holy night, all is calm, all is bright…" Then the light from the Christ candle on the altar is passed, first to the ushers, who pass it to the first person in each row, who in turn pass it to their neighbor. As the light is passed, the room begins to glow. I have the best seat in the house to watch while the sanctuary becomes illuminated as God's children share the light of Christ with one another. Not only does this give me chills, it brings me to tears. Every time. The moment is a striking and visual display of John 1:5: "The light shines in the darkness, and the darkness has not overcome it."

Our world has been walking in darkness since the fall from grace in the garden of Eden. The human children of God have been caught in a war between the opposing forces of darkness and light that have existed since the Creation. Two thousand years ago, God knew that his children were not going to win their battle against the darkness on their own, so God "struck a match"—creating a flame that would ignite the world and the hearts of humankind.

This holy light came to us on a silent night in Bethlehem. And it was prophesied two thousand years earlier in the Book of Numbers, during the latter years of Moses's lifetime. These words from a Cornish hymn tell the intriguing story:

Lo! the Eastern Sages rise,
At a signal from the skies,
Brighter than the brightest gem;
   'Tis the Star of Bethlehem.

Balaam's mystic words appear
Full of light divinely clear;
And the import wrapp'd in them,
   'Tis the Star of Bethlehem.

Joyful let us quickly rise;
Still the signal's in the skies,
David's rod of Jesse's stem,
   'Tis the Star of Bethlehem.[1]

Balaam was a prophet of King Balak of Moab. The king was an enemy of the Israelites, who were making their way through Moab with Moses to the Promised Land. The evil king commanded his prophet to place a curse on Israel. But before he was to pronounce a curse, Balaam was mysteriously moved by a series of events and, instead of a curse, delivered the following prophecy:

> *"I see him, but not now;*
>   *I behold him, but not near.*
> *A star will come out of Jacob;*
>   *a scepter will rise out of Israel.*
>
> . . . .
>
> *A ruler will come out of Jacob."*
>   *(Numbers 24:17, 19)*

Four thousand years ago, the prophet Balaam had a vision of the future, a future that would see the rise of a star and the scepter of a ruler from Israel.

In our previous chapter, we talked about the magi, the wise men from the east, who followed a star to Bethlehem. I mentioned that we don't know with any certainty who these magi were, but Jewish scholars provide an intriguing insight into their possible identity. There is some biblical scholarship and archaeological evidence that suggest the magi were Jewish sages, living in Persia as part of the Diaspora. These scholars of the Torah would have been familiar with the Numbers 24:17 prophecy about the star and scepter coming out of Israel.[2]

Scripture tells us in Matthew 2:1-2, "After Jesus was born in Bethlehem in Judea, during the time of King Herod, Magi from the east came to Jerusalem and asked, 'Where is the one who has been born king of the Jews? We saw his star when it rose and have come to worship him.'"

They saw *his* star. Could it be that when the magi witnessed this eastern star, they understood it to be a fulfillment of the Numbers 24 prophecy? Did they believe this great star to be the manifestation of Adonai's Shekinah—the divine presence of the Almighty—marking the arrival of the Son of Man—the Messiah?[3]

Once again, God brought light into the world, and it was *good*. His light broke into the world that first Christmas in the form of a baby, born in a manger. An everlasting light sent from God to save us from the darkness of sin.

Charles Wesley captured this truth in his famous carol:

> Hark! the herald angels sing,
> "Glory to the newborn King;
> peace on earth, and mercy mild,
> God and sinners reconciled!"

And in verse three:

> Light and life to all he brings,
> risen with healing in his wings.
> Mild he lays his glory by,
> born that we no more may die,
> born to raise us from the earth,
> born to give us second birth.
> Hark! the herald angels sing,
> "Glory to the newborn King!"[4]

It's no surprise that light and Christmas are closely connected. We decorate our Christmas trees, homes, and yards with hundreds of twinkling lights. Across America, towns celebrate the lighting of their community trees. Television news programs cover the lighting of the tree in our nation's capital, accompanied by a story about the tree and the state from which it came.

New York City also competes for recognition for its pageantry at Christmas. A few years ago, Bev and I were at Rockefeller Center when the Christmas tree was lit. That is a night I will always remember. Excitement filled the air as an orchestra played holiday music. Ice skaters, silhouetted by skyscrapers, added to the romance of the evening.

Many of us have family traditions also associated with lights. Christmas lights are an event! Even in the days before social media, word got around. You know, in the original social media: the beauty shop, grocery store, post office. People told one another where to find the special Winter Wonderland kind of streets.

Perhaps it's a tradition in your family to pile into the car and listen to carols as you wind through magical neighborhoods, gazing upon beautiful Christmas lights and decorations. These days, some homes even have spectacular displays synchronized to music that you can tune into on your car radio. (I can't even imagine what their electricity bills are like!)

No matter where you find them, Christmas lights look nice and festive during the daylight hours. But when darkness falls, the lights are dazzling. Light is ever so much more radiant when it pierces the darkness, isn't it?

The prophet Isaiah understood this truth:

> *The people walking in darkness*
> *   have seen a great light;*
> *on those living in the land of deep darkness*
> *   a light has dawned.*
>
> . . . .
>
> *For to us a child is born,*
> *   to us a son is given,*
> *   and the government will be on his shoulders.*
> *And he will be called*
> *   Wonderful Counselor, Mighty God,*
> *   Everlasting Father, Prince of Peace. (9:2, 6)*

Into the darkness of our world came a great light, and his name was Jesus. It is interesting that Jesus used this same imagery when he announced to his followers, "I am the light of the world. Whoever follows me will never walk in darkness, but will have the light of life" (John 8:12).

Jesus did not hide his identity. Rather, he was clear about who he was: God in human flesh, going about his business as the one who brings light, just as he did on the first day the world existed.

As we read through the Gospel accounts, it becomes evident that Jesus came to bring his light to everyone, for we are all precious in his sight. He came for the lonely in our neighborhoods, the ones we know and, especially, the ones we don't know. He came for the strangers, lonely and isolated in a strange land. And he came for the marginalized, the outcasts. And that is some of the darkest territory in which we find people. Those who are ostracized and pushed aside by their own communities, people who feel like they don't belong *anywhere*.

The very night Jesus was born, his ministry began to speak to and bring light to the outcasts. Scripture tells us, "And there were shepherds living out in the fields nearby, keeping watch over their flocks at night. An angel of the Lord appeared to them, and the glory of the Lord shone around them, and they were terrified" (Luke 2:8-9).

Only Luke mentions the shepherds in the story of Jesus's birth. Shepherds were considered the lowest of the low, at the bottom of the Palestinian social ladder. They were smelly men who attended smelly sheep. The Mishnah, Judaism's written record of the oral law, refers to shepherds as incompetent and undeserving of rescue, even if they have fallen into a pit.

How significant it is that God picked these lowly outcasts to be the first ones to hear the joyous news: the Messiah has been born! Even from birth, Christ moved among the lowly. They, not the righteous, were the ones he came to save.[5]

In Jesus's day, the Pharisees considered themselves the elite circle of men who decided who was in and who was out. God was the God of Israel. That's the first circle that determined who was in and who was not. God was not the God of the Gentiles, so they were out. God was the God of the Jews, so they were in.

There were additional circles to be drawn. Within Israel, there was a circle that included only men. And within the circle of men, there was a circle that included only priests. And within the circle of priests, there was a circle in which only the high priest could stand.

But the most important circle, the most essential circle for the Jews to occupy, whether man or woman, priest or layperson, was the circle that divided the unrighteous from the righteous, the circle separating those who were sinners from those who were not.

Sinners were people who didn't keep all the Jewish laws. This included those who ate food that wasn't kosher; those who were diseased or ritually unclean; and those who drank too much, cursed too often, or were too loose with their morals.

There was one thing the Pharisees were certain of: people who were in shouldn't—and didn't—mingle with people who were out.

Interestingly, the word *Pharisees* means "the separated ones." Their goal was to separate from everything and everyone that might make them ritually unclean, impure, or less than righteous. That's how you stay in the circle, and that's how you make sure the undeserving stay out.

In 1871 French archaeologist Charles Simon Clermont-Ganneau discovered a stone that once had stood at the entrance to the temple in Jerusalem. It stated that no outsider should enter the protective enclosure around the sanctuary. And whoever was caught would only have himself to blame for his ensuing death.[6]

This was a warning stone. The sanctuary, the dwelling place of God's presence, had to be protected—from outsiders. God was the God only of Israel.

As we study the New Testament, we quickly recognize that Jesus's entire ministry was to turn this kind of thinking upside down—or rather right side up. In Jesus we find an incredible, revolutionary truth: God has a heart for the outsiders. In fact, we find a God who will go to any length to include the excluded, to embrace the unwanted, and to seek and save the lost.

In Jesus, God erased all the circles that had ever been drawn and drew one huge circle—one big enough for all the sinners and all those whom nobody else wanted. All they have to do is step inside. Women, children, the poor, social outcasts, even Gentiles. In the Gospels we see a Jesus who cares deeply about those who are deemed less important or less deserving in the eyes of others. Over and over again, we see Jesus going out of his way to include those whom everyone else excluded, extending love where it wasn't expected. And many, including his disciples, expressed shock when seeing him do so.

Jesus healed a leper—he actually touched him! He healed a blind man—whom he actually noticed. He forgave the adulteress—he actually spoke to her. He allowed children into his circle. He even broke bread with tax collectors.

Luke records an experience Jesus had as he passed through Jericho. Zacchaeus was a tax collector and a wealthy man. The fact that he worked for Rome made him persona non grata in his community of Jericho in Israel. He was literally shunned by the Jewish community, an outcast, one to avoid by all accounts. When Jesus passed through Jericho, Zacchaeus was eager to see him. He had heard of this prophet and wanted to know about him. Here is what Luke tells us about that encounter:

> *Jesus entered Jericho and was passing through. A man was there by the name of Zacchaeus; he was a chief tax collector and was wealthy. He wanted to see who Jesus was, but because he was short he could not see over the crowd. So he ran ahead and climbed a sycamore-fig tree to see him, since Jesus was coming that way.*
>
> *When Jesus reached the spot, he looked up and said to him, "Zacchaeus, come down immediately. I must stay at your house today." So he came down at once and welcomed him gladly.*
>
> *All the people saw this and began to mutter, "He has gone to be the guest of a sinner."*
>
> *But Zacchaeus stood up and said to the Lord, "Look, Lord! Here and now I give half of my possessions to the poor, and if I have cheated anybody out of anything, I will pay back four times the amount."*
>
> *Jesus said to him, "Today salvation has come to this house, because this man, too, is a son of Abraham. For the Son of Man came to seek and to save the lost." (19:1-10)*

In a single afternoon, Jesus brought his Shekinah light into the life of Zacchaeus, and his followers watched in amazement. But that is who Jesus is, and he expects us to follow in his footsteps: to care for those who are deemed unworthy and those who are living on the margins of society. Matthew records what Jesus clearly laid out for his followers when he announced:

> *"Here's another way to put it: You're here to be light, bringing out the God-colors in the world. God is not a secret to be kept. We're going public with this, as public as a city on a hill. If I make you light-bearers, you don't think I'm going to hide you under a bucket, do you? I'm putting you on a light stand. Now that I've put you there on a hilltop, on a light stand— shine! Keep open house; be generous with your lives. By opening up to others, you'll prompt people to open up with God, this generous Father in heaven." (5:14-16 MSG)*

Jesus tasked us, his followers, with bringing the light of heaven to the dark, malevolent corners of the world, to that thick, black fog many people spend their lives in without knowing how to get out.

Go out and shine your light in the darkness! There is an important aspect of our traditional Sunday services that serves as a weekly reminder of this command. Acolytes are our "light bearers" in the worship service. They carry a flame into the sanctuary ahead of the clergy at the beginning of the service. This flame represents the light of Christ. The Christ candle is lit on the altar and remains lit throughout worship. At the end of the service, the flame from the Christ candle is transferred to the acolyte's taper, and the flame is carried out of the sanctuary, once again going before the clergy and all members of the congregation. The light of Christ leads us out into the world each and every Sunday, reminding us to be reflections of his light in our daily lives and in our communities. It is a light we should not quickly forget as we exit through the church doors on our way to enjoy a family Sunday meal, play a round of golf, or watch a ballgame.

I'm reminded of a particular Sunday that rolls around every year, filled with media hype and expectation: Super Bowl Sunday. In this country it seems that the Super Bowl has become an event known as much for the commercials as for the actual football game.

Certain commercials stay with us. How about the Energizer Bunny? The Geico Gecko? The Chick-fil-A cows? What stands out in my mind are the Motel 6 commercials, featuring the distinctive voice of Tom Bodett, an author, voice actor, and radio host. Each commercial ended with the phrase, "I'm Tom Bodett for Motel 6, and we'll leave the light on for you." Remember that one?

I can't listen to Tom's closing phrase without thinking that this is what we, as Christ's followers, are to be doing: letting our lights shine in a world shrouded in darkness. Light is a universal symbol of hospitality. It's a way of saying that you are welcome here. The very night Jesus was born, a bright star in the heavens announced that the kingdom of God is making room for every man, woman, and child upon the earth.

The light of Christ has been needed in every generation. When Jesus came to earth, there was a lot of darkness—enough darkness that a king attempted to kill him while he was still an infant; enough darkness that religious leaders persecuted him, a friend betrayed him, soldiers mocked and beat him, and a Roman governor ordered his crucifixion. Jesus was an outcast to all but his devoted followers.

In the centuries that followed, there was enough darkness that Roman Christians had to hide and worship in catacombs; enough darkness that Nero would cover their bodies in pitch, set them ablaze, and use them as human torches to light his parties; enough darkness that unwanted babies were left out in the woods to die.

One of those dark times in church history was the period in England when brothers John and Charles Wesley began the Methodist movement. They were living witnesses to a world that was so infused with the oppressive force of darkness that they had to do something about it. When the Methodist movement began, there was enough darkness that ten-year-old boys were hanged for stealing bread because their families had nothing to eat; enough darkness that men and women were bought and sold as nothing more than property; enough darkness that for too long the church did little to protect the poor or speak out against slavery.

Today, our world remains shrouded in darkness. Its characteristics may have changed with the passing of time, but the ever-present enemy of God is still alive and well. Human beings are bought and sold in sexual slave trafficking. Addictions of all kinds are eroding our physical and emotional well-being. Depression and suicide are at epidemic levels.

While we don't have a small circle of Pharisees dictating whom we can and cannot include in our communities, we do live in a society that is quite adept at marginalizing those who are "different," whether it be from physical, cultural, or economic differences. Is it possible they become isolated because we fear them to some extent? Maybe it's because we don't know how to act around them, don't know what to say to them, don't have the resources to care for them, or simply don't know how to help them.

These are the very people Jesus came to earth for. He came to touch them, heal them, speak to them, dine with them, and love them. He came to assure them that there is room for them in his Father's house too. Those on the margins of our societies really need to hear this message. More than anything else, they *want* to be welcomed and included.

To see Jesus's kind of love and inclusion in action is a blessing. Our church has a wonderful ministry that supports the spiritual, physical, and social needs of people with special needs of all ages as well as their family members. It is a powerful thing to see people with special needs find their way in the world using their own unique gifts and talents, guided and encouraged by the love of Christ. One of our special-needs programs is the Resound Choir. Whenever they sing in our worship services there is barely a dry eye in the room, for their faces radiate such pure joy. The light that is consistently and lovingly poured into them pours back out upon us in abundance.

We have another program at our church called Family Promise, which ministers to the local homeless population. Sadly, these people are the lepers of today's society. So often deemed a public nuisance, these men, women, and children are pushed to the very edges of our communities, living under bridges, begging on street corners, sleeping in their cars, or eating scraps of food dug from public trash bins. And when they venture into our midst, they are effectively rendered invisible simply by avoiding eye contact. In 2019, there were a half million of these invisible, homeless outcasts living in the United States.

Family Promise houses homeless families, helping them get back on their feet. If you ask any of our members who serve in this ministry, they will tell you that the homeless people they are serving are *not* lazy. Rarely is that their problem. The issues that led to their homelessness are complex. Many of them just need a helping hand so they can get back on their feet and back into a safe place to call home.

These ministries are but two examples of the many ways God's light can pierce the darkness of another person's life.

Most all of us have heard the remarkable story of Helen Keller. Helen was born a bright and happy child in Tuscumbia, Alabama, in 1880. But when she was nineteen months old, an unknown illness tragically left her permanently blind and deaf. The next five years were incredibly difficult for Helen and her parents, as they struggled to deal with the daily challenges of living with a physically handicapped child. Helen became precocious and unruly, subjecting their household to frequent and violent tantrums. Certainly, Helen was frightened and lost in the complete darkness of her new reality. Finally, the Kellers reached out for help. They searched for a governess to work with their daughter, and in March 1887, a "miracle worker" entered the Keller household. Twenty-year-old Anne Sullivan, a graduate of Perkins Institute for the Blind, began to work with her new six-year-old charge. This was a life-changing event for both Helen and Anne, who became lifelong friends. Their story is poignantly told in the 1962 film *The Miracle Worker*, starring Patty Duke and Anne Bancroft.

As Anne Sullivan worked with her young student, she realized that Helen was extremely gifted. Under Anne's tutelage, Helen learned to read, write, and then speak. This accomplishment was so extraordinary that American writer Mark Twain dubbed Anne Sullivan as a "miracle worker." As the years went by, Helen made remarkable progress and fulfilled her dream to attend college. She attended Radcliffe College and in 1904 became the first deaf-blind person ever to graduate with a Bachelor of Arts degree. Helen eventually became a celebrated author, speaker, and political and social activist supporting the needs of those suffering from loss of vision as well as supporting the causes of women's suffrage and worker's rights.[7]

The constant company of her faithful teacher for much of her life was a source of joy for Helen. She once said this about Anne: "Gradually I got used to the silence and darkness that surrounded me and forgot that it had ever been different, until she came—my teacher—who was to set my spirit free."[8]

Anne Sullivan was plagued with serious vision problems of her own, yet she worked faithfully and diligently to bring Helen out of her darkness so she could fully participate in the world. This is what Christ does for us. His light breaks into the thick fog of our darkness as he proclaims his good news and sets us free.

When Bev and I take groups to Israel, we always include Yad Vashem, the World Holocaust Remembrance Center, on the itinerary. It is a stunning architectural achievement set in the forested hillsides just outside of Jerusalem. No one can walk through this expansive museum without being horrified at humanity's capacity for evil. But what caught my attention on one particular visit were the trees lining the pathways that wind through the Yad Vashem complex. Hundreds of trees have been planted to honor "The Righteous Among the Nations," non-Jews who took great risks to save Jews during the Holocaust. They are also known as "righteous Gentiles." As I walked the paths and looked at the markers, I recognized several names, including Oskar Schindler, Raoul Wallenberg, and Corrie ten Boom.

Corrie was a Dutch watchmaker who lived in her family home in the Netherlands with her father, Casper, and sister Betsie. A Christian family, they made their home a hiding place for Jews during the Nazi occupation and World War II. The ten Boom family helped many Jews escape the terror of the Nazi regime.

Eventually, they were betrayed and imprisoned for their roles in protecting Jews. Corrie and Betsie were sent to the Vught Transit Camp in the Netherlands and from there to the Ravensbrück women's labor camp in Germany. Toward the end of the war, the camp population at Ravensbrück grew to more than ten times the originally planned number. Imprisoned women were forced to work in many kinds of slave labor and were hardly fed. Living conditions were deplorable almost beyond description.

One morning, Corrie awoke with a bad cold. Without so much as a handkerchief for her runny nose, she felt she simply could not bear it. "Why don't you pray for a hankie?" Betsie asked. Corrie almost laughed! Here they were, surrounded by unspeakable suffering and death, and her sister suggested praying for a *handkerchief*! Betsie, however, was not deterred by her sister's lack of faith. She prayed a simple prayer in the name of Jesus, asking for a hankie because Corrie had a bad cold. Corrie just shook her head and walked away.

A short time later, a fellow prisoner who worked in the camp hospital approached Corrie and held out a small package, saying, "I bring you a little present." When Corrie opened it, she found a handkerchief! She asked the woman, "Did Betsie tell you? Did you know I had a cold?" The woman responded, "I know nothing. I was busy sewing handkerchiefs out of an old piece of sheet, and there was a voice in my heart saying, 'Take a hankie to Corrie ten Boom.' So, there is your gift, from God."

When telling this story later, Corrie commented, "That pocket handkerchief, made from an old piece of sheet, was a message from heaven for me. It told me that there is a heavenly Father who hears if one of His children on this planet prays for even just a little thing like a hankie."[9]

Although her sister Betsie was put to death, Corrie survived the death camp and went on to become an author and inspirational speaker. Her most famous book, *The Hiding Place*, was also turned into a 1975 film.

This is a story about how two people became lights in the deadly darkness of the Holocaust. Corrie ten Boom and her family opened their home at great personal risk to give the gift of God's love and life to the many Jews they hid from the Nazis. And the prisoner who worked at the Ravensbrück death camp hospital brought a great light to the heart of a sick and discouraged Corrie when she delivered a simple handkerchief. Because she listened to and obeyed God's whisper in her heart, she brought to Corrie the knowledge that God indeed had not forgotten her and had heard her prayers.

Much like those in Nazi Europe, those today who are physically and mentally disabled, homeless, persecuted, and imprisoned would have been the ones to fall outside the circle of inclusion drawn by the Pharisees. They were the outcasts. But all of these outcasts fall inside the circle drawn by Jesus, because he sees them in a completely different way. He sees them as lost, something of great value that needs to be found. And the heart of God is always tuned to hear the cries of the lost.

Bev and I love to watch movies with our grandchildren. There's nothing like watching a classic story we grew up with come to life on the big screen for a new generation, and Disney does it so well with their animated versions. *The Hunchback of Notre Dame* is one of those movies, based on Victor Hugo's classic novel of the same name. It is the powerful story of Quasimodo, a hunchbacked young man who lives in the bell tower of Notre Dame Cathedral and falls in love with a beautiful young Roma woman named Esmeralda.

Both are shunned by society: Quasimodo because of his distorted, frightening appearance and Esmeralda because of her family. The Roma, who were sometimes called Gypsies, were despised in parts of Europe.

In one touching scene, the young Esmeralda is running for her life, fleeing from the villains who are trying to capture her. She takes refuge inside Notre Dame Cathedral, and there she pours out her heart to God in prayer. She confesses to God that she is a social outcast and may not have the right to address God. But she has a sense that God, through Jesus, knows what it feels like to be an outcast. And that God cares about the outcasts. She asks God to help those who are poor, those who receive no mercy from the privileged of society, and those who are shunned. *Are we not all children of God?* she wonders. Would God look on her and her people and believe they are God's children as well? She sings "God Help the Outcasts" (lyrics by Stephen Schwartz, from *The Hunchback of Notre Dame* soundtrack, Walt Disney Music Company, 1996), which asks God, "Were you once an outcast too?"

Esmeralda's cry in "God Help the Outcasts" that she thought all people are "the children of God" hits close to home, doesn't it? It should, because it points to an important truth—each person is valuable to God.

Young Esmeralda and her heartfelt plea remind me of another young woman, this one in Bethlehem. I wonder if Jesus's love for those shunned and marginalized by the community evoked a tender reminder of the treatment of his own mother and father? Mary and Joseph were unwed parents, which would have placed them in that circle of exclusion. They, too, understood the heartbreak of being outcasts. I wonder if, as she nursed Jesus, Mary whispered into his tiny ear, "Always love everyone. All people matter to God."

The Book of Hosea presents us with a poignant insight into this truth that all people are of great value to God, no matter what their circumstances are. Hosea tells a love story with a twist featuring a faithful husband (the prophet Hosea) and his adulterous wife (Gomer). Hosea is told by God to marry the known prostitute Gomer and to have children with her. Hosea obeys and has three children. The first, a son, is named Jezreel, meaning "scattering." The second, a daughter, is named Lo-Ruhamah, meaning "not loved." The third child, another son, was named Lo-Ammi, meaning "not my people."

At first reading this sounds like an odd, sad story. But the story of this marriage is symbolic of God's relationship with the unfaithful children of Israel. The names of Hosea and Gomer's children prophetically described what was to come of Israel: they would be scattered in exile because they did not keep the covenants required to be God's people.

As the story goes on, Gomer continued in her adulterous activities during the marriage and a separation followed. But Hosea, whose name means "salvation," persisted in his love for this woman, who was an outcast and a sinner. Since she was no longer considered his wife and was powerless to save herself, he bought her back for fifteen shekels of silver and about four hundred pounds of barley, restoring her honor and her position.

Hosea's actions to redeem his unfaithful wife are symbolic of the sacrificial and redeeming love God has for his people, his children. Gomer needed the redeeming love and light of her husband. Israel needed the redeeming love and light of God.

God does indeed love the outcasts—the least, the last, and the lost—so much so that he sent his only son on that first Christmas to conduct an all-out search to bring the outcasts home. As Jesus shined his Shekinah light into the darkness of our world, the truth of our human condition was revealed. All of us are outcasts, for every single one of us is a sinner who has fallen from grace. We are outcasts from the kingdom of heaven without the redemption of our Father through Jesus and the cross.

I think that is why our Christmas Eve service is so meaningful to me. From my place on the altar, I look out and behold a sea of people standing shoulder to shoulder and hand in hand. This is what God ordained for us. We need one another. We need to pass the light, one to another, in order to pierce the darkness of our world. We are all outcasts, and none of us can find our way home alone. But God left a light on for us.

As the flame from the Christ candle is passed, the room becomes filled with light. And as we sing, our voices are carried straight to the throne of the source of that light.

> Silent night, holy night,
> Son of God, love's pure light;
> radiant beams from thy holy face
> with the dawn of redeeming grace,
> Jesus, Lord, at thy birth,
> Jesus, Lord, at thy birth.[10]

4

WALK EACH OTHER HOME

"Father, I want those you have given me to be with me where I am."
(John 17:24)

Like many a young child, growing up I was fascinated by Daniel Defoe's tale of *Robinson Crusoe*. I can remember falling asleep at night reading that book. Perhaps you are familiar with the story. A headstrong young man ignores his family's advice and leaves his comfortable home in England for a life at sea. But a shipwreck tosses young Robinson overboard into stormy waters. He washes up on a remote island, which he calls the Island of Despair, and lives there for twenty-eight years as a castaway.

What an apt name for both the island and for the emotional state of Robinson Crusoe. Can you imagine the depths of his loneliness? Crusoe's despair is so deep that he begins talking to his parrot and other animals, only to find that they could not appease his yearning for human contact. As a young boy I was haunted by that story of being lost at sea with no hope of rescue.

I've never been stranded on a remote island, but I have been lost. Perhaps you have too. I'm not talking about the simple discovery that you've made a wrong turn and suddenly find yourself taking an unfamiliar route. I'm talking about finding yourself really and truly lost. Unable to find your bearings at all. It is a terribly frightening feeling.

One lovely fall afternoon when Bev and I were in college and dating, we drove to Natural Bridge State Resort Park in eastern Kentucky for a picnic. I found the place enchanting. From the top of the famed magnificent sandstone arch, which is surrounded by the Daniel Boone National Forest, you have a 360-degree view of colorful, distant ridges and lush green valleys.

Coming from the windswept prairies of West Texas, I had never experienced the stunning beauty of fall foliage. We could not have chosen a more romantic setting to watch the sun set behind the mountains. What we did not consider, however, is how quickly twilight would turn to night. By the time we decided to gather our belongings and hike back to the car, darkness had completely engulfed us. Nothing was visible, and we could not find the narrow hiking path which led back to the ranger station and the small parking lot. Fear quickly replaced those loving feelings, and we realized we might be stuck on the mountain until dawn. As we attempted to "crawl" our way down, we became disoriented and more lost. Our situation seemed hopeless until at last, in the distance, we spotted a park ranger with his search light. Hallelujah! Answered prayers!

No one wants to be lost. No one wants to be overcome by the despair of thinking, even for a moment, that they might never get home again. It is a terrible feeling. But sadly, that is the story of every one of us. Since Adam and Eve left the garden of Eden, humankind has been wandering, spiritually lost in the wilderness, looking for the way back home.

Two thousand years ago in Bethlehem, a brilliant star in the eastern night sky announced to the world that help had arrived. God sent a search party, a party of one, to rescue us from our darkness. And that was our Savior, Jesus, the one who stepped from his throne of glory and humbled himself to be born and live among us.

> O little town of Bethlehem,
> how still we see thee lie;
> above thy deep and dreamless sleep
> the silent stars go by.
> Yet in thy dark streets shineth
> the everlasting light;
> the hopes and fears of all the years
> are met in thee tonight.[1]

It's no wonder we celebrate the season of Advent with such joy and expectation. We who are lost have been found! We are profoundly loved, and our Savior has come to walk us back home.

As Scripture says, "For God so loved the world that he gave his one and only Son, that whoever believes in him shall not perish but have eternal life. For God did not send his Son into the world to condemn the world, but to save the world through him" (John 3:16-17).

God sent Jesus to lead humankind out of spiritual darkness and into an inheritance of hope. This rescue mission wasn't just the reason for Christ's birth; it also shaped his entire ministry. Jesus came for the least, the last, and the lost children of his world. When criticized by the Pharisees, the religious elite, for associating with sinners and outcasts, Jesus said to them, "It is not the healthy who need a doctor, but the sick. I have not come to call the righteous, but sinners" (Mark 2:17). And in Luke 19:10 Jesus proclaimed, "For the Son of Man came to seek and to save the lost."

On one occasion, when tax collectors were gathering around to hear Jesus teach, Pharisees and teachers of the law began muttering, "This man welcomes sinners and eats with them" (Luke 15:2). Jesus responded to their complaint by telling a story about a sheep who had wandered away from a fold of one hundred. Jesus looked at his accusers and asked something like, "Wouldn't any shepherd worth his salt leave the ninety-nine sheep who have not wandered away to go in search of the one lost sheep? And wouldn't that same shepherd, upon finding that one sheep, put it on his shoulders and call his friends together to rejoice with him because he has found the sheep that was lost?" Jesus closed his rebuttal by stating: "I tell you that in the same way there will be more rejoicing in heaven over one sinner who repents than over ninety-nine righteous persons who do not need to repent" (v. 7).

To illustrate this further, Jesus proceeded to tell a parable of a lost son. I imagine many of us are familiar with this story. The younger of two sons asked his father for his share of his inheritance early. In that day and time this would have been similar to wishing that his father might drop dead; a grievous insult. Leaving home, the younger son traveled to a distant country and lost all of his inheritance. The son hit rock bottom, so to speak. He became so desperate that he wished he could eat the food given to the pigs. Finally, he decided that his only option was to return home and beg his father to take him back as a lowly servant. So, he got up and went to his father.

Can you imagine the young man's anxiety as he walked up the lane to his childhood home? Would his father receive him back? Would he lash out in anger? To the young son's astonishment, he finds his father running down the road to greet him with open arms.

> *"But while he was still a long way off, his father saw him and was filled with compassion for him; he ran to his son, threw his arms around him and kissed him.*

> *"The son said to him, 'Father, I have sinned against heaven and against you. I am no longer worthy to be called your son.'*

> *"But the father said to his servants, 'Quick! Bring the best robe and put it on him. Put a ring on his finger and sandals on his feet. Bring the fattened calf and kill it. Let's have a feast and celebrate. For this son of mine was dead and is alive again; he was lost and is found.' So they began to celebrate." (vv. 20-24)*

But the older son, who had been loyal and faithful to his father, became angry and complained. "'My son,' the father said, 'you are always with me, and everything I have is yours. But we had to celebrate and be glad, because this brother of yours was dead and is alive again; he was lost and is found'" (vv. 31-32).

I suspect each of us can relate to these stories. Some of us, like the sheep, are lost because we have wandered away from our

Shepherd. Perhaps the search for greener grass and freedom of choice has led us down one wrong path after another until we have found ourselves hopelessly lost. Or, like the younger son, maybe we let pride, arrogance, and an ungrateful spirit cause us to rebel. We forget who we are and whose we are.

All of us need to be rescued. Whether we've wandered away gradually, like the lost sheep, or we've demanded to live our own way, like the wayward son, we all need to be found. Scripture says, "All have sinned and fall short of the glory of God, and all are justified freely by his grace through the redemption that came by Christ Jesus" (Romans 3:23-24).

Adam and Eve might have eaten that first forbidden fruit in the garden, tempted as they were by the adversary, but every person born since also has endured temptation and fallen short. Every single one of us has turned astray.

In the United Methodist tradition, we recognize this truth every time we approach the Lord's Table to celebrate Holy Communion. We pray, confessing:

> Merciful God,
> we confess that we have not loved you with our whole heart.
> We have failed to be an obedient church.
> We have not done your will,
> we have broken your law,
> we have rebelled against your love,
> we have not loved our neighbors,
> and we have not heard the cry of the needy.

Forgive us, we pray.
Free us for joyful obedience,
through Jesus Christ our Lord. Amen.[2]

Thank goodness for a loving God who does not want any of us to remain lost in our sin, rebellion, and disobedience. Thank goodness for a God who wants to forgive us and free us to walk with God. The imagery Jesus uses in the parables of the lost sheep and lost son reveals an important insight. The shepherd goes out in search of the one lost sheep, and when he finds it, he puts it on his shoulders and walks the sheep back into the fold. And then he celebrates.

In the parable of the lost son, the father keeps a lookout for his lost son—he never loses hope. And when he sees him, far off down the road, the father runs to his son and embraces him. He walks his son back home. And then he celebrates.

Find those who are lost. Walk them home. Time and time again, Jesus taught and demonstrated this during his ministry. Just as he taught in parables, he also provided people with visual testimonies of his power and authority through the miracles that he performed. In each instance, Jesus did not just heal people for the sake of healing them; he did so in order to restore them to a right relationship with God and others. Jesus reinstated these people into the community. The man at the pool of Bethesda, the woman who had been bleeding for twelve years, the man with leprosy, the men who were blind, the people possessed by demons—all of these would have been considered outcasts in Jesus's time. Their conditions rendered them "unclean" and unworthy to live among the general population of their community.

So Jesus not only cured them but also enabled them to rejoin society. This is the truth we discover in the parables of the lost sheep and the lost son. They are not just found. They are returned to community, and they are celebrated.

This was so important to Jesus that, toward the end of his earthly ministry, he gave both a command and a commission to his followers. "A new command I give you: Love one another. As I have loved you, so you must love one another" (John 13:34). And just before his Ascension, Jesus issued his Great Commission to his disciples: "All authority in heaven and on earth has been given to me. Therefore go and make disciples of all nations, baptizing them in the name of the Father and of the Son and of the Holy Spirit, and teaching them to obey everything I have commanded you. And surely I am with you always, to the very end of the age" (Matthew 28:18-20).

Jesus was calling those followers, and all that came after them, into community.

Let's think again about that first Christmas: a night that should have been ordinary but, in fact, became the pivot around which all of human history turns. I imagine that the poor humble shepherds could scarcely take in the wonder of a God who would be born as a tiny, helpless baby. I imagine they felt profound awe at the realization that God would come down from heaven to dwell among even them, men who lived on the outskirts of society.

When you think about it, of course it makes sense that Jesus was born in a humble abode, laid in a manger, and attended by those whom society deemed unimportant. Where else can the light of Christ shine as brightly as in those places where the need is greatest? That blessed night, God showed us all not only that we are worth searching for but also to what length he would go to bring us back home.

Jesus didn't come only to find us and bring us home himself. He also came to call us into community as people of faith. We have God always, but also, we have one another. And Jesus knew that we would need one another.

Have you ever heard the phrase "bowling alone"? It has become a kind of shorthand expression for the autonomous, highly individualistic nature of society. Robert Putnam, a sociologist, coined the phrase in 1995 in a relatively obscure academic journal. Putnam noticed that community engagement in America was declining steadily, and this observation resonated with people. It certainly resonated with me. I thought, *Yes, something has changed. Something has happened in our country over the past few decades. People aren't connecting these days, not like they used to.*

Putnam's point was that, although we might be bowling just as much as in years past, people were less likely to do so in organized leagues. In fact, he found this to be true of political parties, PTAs, labor unions, fraternal organizations, and churches, concluding that declining levels of participation are evident in every area of civic life.

Five years later, Putnam released a book about his study titled— you guessed it—*Bowling Alone*.[3] The book became a nationwide best seller, yet it did not seem to do much to reverse the trend. Twenty years later, we still seem to be "bowling alone"—and now, even worse, we are "virtually bowling" from the comfort of our own homes using video-game technology.[4]

Again, consider that first Christmas. The story is steeped in human interaction. The innkeeper, although perhaps unable to offer a standard room, provided Mary and Joseph with a safe and warm place to welcome their precious son into the world. Certainly, this innkeeper must have provided for them in the days that followed. Mary and Joseph welcomed the shepherds and, later, welcomed wise men who came from afar to worship this infant Lord. The wise men brought gifts and provisions. Against all odds, an unlikely little community was formed that enabled those new parents to catch their breath and prepare for the arduous journey that lay ahead.

The Christmas story, and the life and ministry of Jesus, teach us that following Christ is not intended to be a lone-ranger experience. We are not meant to journey back home alone. One of the first things Jesus did when he began his public ministry was to create a community out of a ragtag bunch of people—at first fishermen, then a tax collector, also faithful women, including one from whom Jesus drove out seven demons. Jesus invited these people, and more, to follow him—to walk together, eat together, travel together, and learn together as he showed them the true importance of belonging to a community of faith.

God's rescue mission goes beyond just "finding" us and bringing us back to his heart. God also restores us in our relationships with one another. Community is integral to living a life of faith. We need God. We need the grace and mercy God offers us through faith in Jesus Christ. We need God to work within us through the presence and power of the Holy Spirit. But we also need one another.

As a pastor, I come across a number of people who tell me that they don't need the church. One such person said to me that he doesn't attend worship on Sunday mornings because he communes with God while riding his beloved Harley motorcycle. Now, I'll concede that if I spent any time riding a motorcycle on the streets and highways of Houston, I would be praying too! But this man's comment, and the others I've heard like it, illustrate a "bowling alone" mentality. We've lost an appreciation for reaching outside of our comfort zones and truly connecting with other people. Even where religion is concerned, most people in society seem more interested in cultivating their own personal spirituality than in committing to organized religion in any form. Increasingly, people are saying, "I can do it alone."

I know that at times organized religion and faith-based communities have made a mess of things. And those failures have taken a toll on the religious landscape of America. Church attendance is dropping at an alarming rate. "Over the last decade, the share of Americans who say they attend religious services at least once or twice a month dropped by 7 percentage points, while the share who say they attend religious services less often (if at all) has risen by the same degree." American adults describing themselves as Christian is down 12 percentage points over the past decade. Meanwhile, the religiously unaffiliated share of the population, consisting of people who describe their religious identity as atheist, agnostic, or "nothing in particular," now stands at 26 percent, up from 17 percent in 2009.[5]

A growing number of Americans profess spirituality but report they are not religious.[6] Many seem to be saying, "I love Jesus but not the church."

Perhaps we can enjoy meaningful fellowship with God on a walk through the woods, kneeling in the garden, or even riding a motorcycle. But none of those things encourage us to live outside of ourselves. Practicing spiritual disciplines like meditation, prayer, reading the Bible, and spending time in solitude are essential to our faith. But the God of the Bible is a communal God. God makes himself known in common space, on common ground. God always calls us into relationship with one another, even as we grow in our relationship with him.

So, to say that we don't need community to commune with God is like saying we can cure our own diseases without seeking help. It's like saying that doctors and hospitals are too organized. At some point, isolation will stunt our spiritual growth because it is our interactions with other people through which God refines and matures our faith.

And quite frankly, we believers also need one another for accountability and encouragement. The author of Hebrews writes, "Let us consider how we may spur one another on toward love and good deeds, not giving up meeting together, as some are in the habit of doing, but encouraging one another" (10:24-25). The apostle Paul urges us to "encourage one another and build each other up, just as in fact you are doing" (1 Thessalonians 5:11). In Galatians he admonishes us to "carry each other's burdens" (6:2).

Why? Because they knew, as did Jesus, that the road of faith would not always be easy. Jesus said, "In this world you will have trouble" (John 16:33). Most of us probably know this to be true. We know that some days the going will be smooth, the path straight, the sun shining, and we will walk with a spring in our step. But on other days, we will encounter rocks, potholes, detours, and dead ends. We will veer off course, like the lost sheep, and find ourselves in unfamiliar surroundings, unsure of how to get back to the fold. There will be other days when we are exhausted, worn out from the realities of earthly life, and unable to make it one inch further. Our knees will buckle, and we will collapse. But if we rely on one another, in all of those instances we will have tangible arms and hands to help pick us back up, to carry us at times, to hold our hands, and to stop and wait for us to regain our strength. If we rely on one another, if we will choose to "bowl together," the path becomes a little easier.

Some years ago, Bev and I traveled to California for vacation. It was our first visit to that beautiful state. Of course, we wanted to drive the famous Highway 1, which hugs the Pacific coastline. Another must-see for us was the Muir Woods National Monument, just north of San Francisco. Though I had seen photographs of the giant coastal redwood trees, I was not prepared for the impact of viewing them in person. They are awe-inspiring! The tallest trees tower as high as three hundred feet above the ground. That is as tall as a thirty-one-story building.

What we learned from the park ranger is that, surprisingly, these massive trees are sustained by shallow root systems. Their roots reach out in all directions to capture the greatest amount of moisture. While this gives them access to the water they need to survive, it does not help them withstand heavy winds. But the ranger pointed out that in the California forest the redwoods grow together in clusters, allowing the trees' root systems to intertwine, providing support for one another. Only together can these giants survive the forces of nature. A lone tree would quickly fall to high winds and raging floods.[7]

In much the same way, when believers gather together, we provide support for one another. When we face our own storms of pain and suffering, doubt and despair, our faith survives because our roots intertwine, allowing us to draw strength from one another. God calls us into community for this purpose: so that we can lift one another up, rejoice and grieve with one another, pray for one another, stand up for one another, and when necessary speak the truth to one another in love. We are to be the hands and feet of Christ reaching out to the world and also to each other. What I know for sure is that we need each other more than we realize.

And let's remember that we are all journeying to the same place: home to the arms of God. So, we might as well join hands and help one another get there.

There is an event that is seared into my memory as one of the most moving examples of Christian community that I have personally experienced. It came in the wake of a devastating storm: a Category 4 hurricane named Harvey.

Hurricane Harvey made landfall along the southern Texas coastline on August 25, 2017. Inflicting damages of about $125 billion, Harvey is "the second-most costly hurricane to hit the U.S. mainland since 1900."[8]

After making landfall, the storm stalled over the Houston area, dumping an unprecedented sixty inches of rain in four days—an entire year's worth of rain. I developed a new appreciation for Noah during that storm!

According to a California geophysicist, the sheer weight of the water covering the greater Houston area caused the earth's crust to temporarily sink two centimeters (about one inch). This historic flooding event affected thirteen million people. Nearly 135,000 homes were damaged or destroyed, and up to a million cars were wrecked. And because the floodwaters extended way beyond the established 100- and 500-year flood plains, most of the affected were uninsured.[9]

Rescue and relief efforts were challenging. Water was everywhere, indiscriminately cutting off entire neighborhoods from access, while other neighborhoods stayed relatively accessible.

Thankfully, our church remained accessible. While the storm was still raging, a skeleton staff at the church was busy making arrangements for disaster relief with local, county, state, and national officials. The Woodlands United Methodist Church was made the South Montgomery County Distribution Center for disaster relief supplies. Because of the catastrophic nature of this storm, we knew the needs of the community were going to be far beyond what we could imagine. So, an e-mail message was sent out to all the church members listing the kinds of donations that were needed and directing that they be dropped off at the church. Unbelievably, within fifteen minutes after that message went out, cars began pouring into the church parking lot with donations—while the dangerous storm was still pouring flooding rain all around them.

In the following weeks, I witnessed a different kind of flood—a flood of compassion in the form of the hands and feet of Jesus Christ.

Our gymnasium was converted into a stockroom and "store." Here, storm victims could shop for much-needed items including food, clothing, shoes, pet food and supplies, children's toys and books, diapers, bedding, school supplies, personal hygiene items, and cleaning supplies. Walmart gift cards were distributed to each family that came seeking assistance.

Donations poured in from all over the country. Eighteen-wheeler trucks pulled into our parking lot, filled with food products and bottled water. Fifteen cars and two fifth-wheel camper trailers were donated.

Over the next six weeks, six thousand volunteers from our church family and the surrounding community served the needs of nearly two thousand families. They guided them through our distribution center, listened to their stories, and prayed with them. They mucked out houses, tearing out carpeting and removing damaged drywall. In cooperation with Habitat for Humanity, they helped begin the rebuilding process. This process, incidentally, is continuing three years later.

Of all these amazing interactions of a community coming together to be the hands and feet of Christ, one in particular stands out. It is the story of Morris Reinisch and his wife, Barbara. They experienced flood damage to their home during the hurricane. Relatively new to town and with no family in the area, they needed help but didn't know where to find it.

Volunteers from our church happened to be next-door to the Reinisch home, helping one of our church families who had also taken in flood water.

Our volunteers noticed that no one was working at Morris and Barbara's house. So, they went over and knocked on their door. When

Morris and Barbara opened the door, they were astonished to hear our church members announce, "We're here to help."

Within a few hours a large team of our volunteers arrived. They mucked. They removed soggy drywall, and they showed up day after day. They washed dishes. They moved furniture. They cleaned. They did whatever was needed to serve the needs of this couple. One of our volunteers even gave Morris and Barbara a bag of provisions, with a Scripture verse inside.

Morris kept the verse. Over the next several months, he kept thinking, *I've got to go to that church. I want to see for myself what kind of crazy church would send people to love on complete strangers.*

Some months later, Morris did show up at our church and attended a worship service. At the conclusion of that service, Morris introduced himself to Harvest Pastor Mark Sorensen, saying abruptly, "Hi, I'm Morris, and I'm Jewish." Pastor Sorensen responded, "Well, hi. I'm Mark." And at that moment, a friendship began to develop.

Morris had questions—many questions. (He is a lawyer.) Over the next several months, Morris and Mark began meeting together for coffee. Morris brought pages of questions to each meeting. They talked about faith and the Bible. After many fruitful conversations, on October 13, 2019, Morris was baptized by Pastor Mark during a Harvest worship service. He professed his faith in our Jesus as his Savior and was joyfully celebrated as the newest member in our community of faith.

This was a powerful illustration of Jesus's call to be in community with one another, loving our neighbor and sharing the good news of Jesus Christ.

As we experience the impact of Christian community in our lives, we recognize the importance of Christian believers who guide and prepare us to receive the grace of God—just as Mark Sorensen took the time to guide Morris into the community of faith.

I mentioned one of my writing assistants earlier in this book, Kimberly Constant. I first met her when she was serving as a pastoral intern at our church as she was finishing seminary. But I learned that Kimberly and her family had been part of our church for some time. In fact, a decade or so before we met, Kimberly and her husband had moved to Texas from California, and on their first Sunday in town they showed up at our church. As a parent of a new baby girl, Kimberly said she knew she needed to get connected to God if she was going to have a shot at getting the "parenting gig" right. What Kimberly didn't know was how much she needed our community. She did not grow up attending church, and like many people, eschewed the idea that she needed help from anywhere or anyone—until she had a baby. She decided to join a women's Bible study where she was mentored in the faith by godly women who encouraged her.

Over time, Kimberly realized that she was no longer coming just "for the kids." Something was resonating within her. That was the beginning of her faith journey, one which eventually led her to seminary and into ministry. Ask her today and she will tell you that it was that community of women who loved and nurtured her that made all the difference.

Most people, I assume, have heard of Reverend Billy Graham, who, during his evangelistic crusades, delivered the good news to nearly 215 million people around the globe. Interestingly, Graham did not grow up wanting to be a preacher. Far from it. He grew up on a dairy farm near Charlotte, North Carolina. As a teenager, he was resentful of his family's worship and Bible-reading practices and attended church grudgingly.

Around Graham's sixteenth birthday, a traveling evangelical preacher named Dr. Mordecai Ham held a series of revival meetings in Charlotte. The evangelist preached six days a week, morning and night, for eleven weeks. And he didn't mince words about sin.

"Everything I heard or read about him made me feel antagonistic toward the whole affair," Graham shared in his autobiography. "It sounded like a religious circus to me."[10]

Billy's parents attended the meetings, but their enthusiasm didn't rub off on their teenage son. "I did not want anything to do with anyone called an evangelist—and particularly with such a colorful character as Dr. Ham," Graham said. "I told my parents that I would not go to hear him."[11] But a series of events during this eleven-week period piqued Graham's curiosity to the point that one night he attended one of Ham's revival services—and he was spellbound. All he could recall about that night was that he heard a voice, in addition to Ham's. It was the voice of the Holy Spirit. And just a few days shy of his sixteenth birthday, Graham answered Mordecai Ham's altar call.

Reflecting on that life-changing night, Graham said that he "walked down to the front, feeling as if I had lead weights attached to my feet." Looking around, he saw a woman next to him with tears running down her cheeks. "I did not feel any special emotion of any kind just then," he said, and wondered if he was making a fool of himself. "I almost turned around and went back to my seat."[12]

It was then that a family friend came beside Graham, told him about God's plan for salvation, prayed for him, and prayed along with him as Graham received Christ.

It made a great difference to Graham's experience that someone walked alongside him as he made this life-changing decision. In his future crusades, Graham made sure that trained counselors accompanied those who came forward at the invitation. Graham had learned the importance of having someone help walk us home.[13]

We need each other more than we realize. Scripture records that "in Christ we, though many, form one body, and each member belongs to all the others" (Romans 12:5). As the body of Christ, each of us has been given different gifts designed not only to complement one another but also to draw us together and to render us dependent on one another and on Jesus Christ as our Lord.

As his final Passover meal came to an end, Jesus turned his face to heaven and prayed to his Father on behalf of his beloved community of disciples. It is one of the most beautiful prayers in Scripture, and it is found in the seventeenth chapter of John.

> "I have given them the glory you gave me, so they may be one as we are one. I am in them and you are in me. May they experience such perfect unity that the world will know that you sent me and that you love them as much as you love me. Father, I want these whom you have given me to be with me where I am. Then they can see all the glory you gave me because you loved me even before the world began!"
>
> *(vv. 22-24 NLT)*

There is a spark of the divine nature in each of us, for we were created in God's image and are intimately connected to Jesus. Perhaps at this time of year, during Advent, this divine spark creates a yearning for us to connect with one another in especially meaningful ways. And when we reach out to one another in love and community, we connect with our Savior. In truth, we are family.

The Advent season is that cherished time of year when we love to gather together with our families to celebrate the wondrous miracle of Christmas: the miracle that Jesus came to earth to walk us back home to our heavenly Father. And perhaps one of the most intriguing ways to tell the Christmas story comes from Scripture that takes place not in Bethlehem but near Jerusalem on Easter Sunday.

Luke 24 tells the story of two of Jesus's followers as they made their way down the road to the small village of Emmaus. It was Easter afternoon, and they were discussing the distressing events of the past three days. Jesus, their beloved friend and rabbi, had been sentenced to death and crucified. They had witnessed the power of his ministry and believed he was to be their redeemer, their long-awaited Messiah. But now he was dead. And to make things worse, his body was missing! Just that morning, some of the women from their group had gone to visit Jesus's tomb and found it empty. They made the impossible claim that an angel told them that Jesus was alive! Several of their companions raced to the tomb to see if what the women had said was true. Indeed, Jesus was not there. He was nowhere to be found.

As the two men walked the road to Emmaus, commiserating with each other, trying to make sense of it all, they were joined by a stranger. It was Jesus himself, but they did not recognize him. As he walked alongside them, Jesus noticed their obvious distress and asked them what they were discussing.

> They stood still, their faces downcast. One of them, named Cleopas, asked him, "Are you the only one visiting Jerusalem who does not know the things that have happened there in these days?"
>
> "What things?" he asked.
>
> "About Jesus of Nazareth," they replied. (vv. 17-19)

Jesus listened as Cleopas and his friend shared with him all that had transpired. When they finished, he said to them,

> "How foolish you are, and how slow to believe all that the prophets have spoken! Did not the Messiah have to suffer these things and then enter his glory?" And beginning with Moses and all the Prophets, he explained to them what was said in all the Scriptures concerning himself.
>
> As they approached the village to which they were going, Jesus continued on as if he were going farther. But they urged him strongly, "Stay with us, for it is nearly evening; the day is almost over." So he went in to stay with them.
>
> When he was at the table with them, he took bread, gave thanks, broke it and began to give it to them. Then their eyes were opened and they recognized him, and he disappeared from their sight. They asked each other, "Were not our hearts burning within us while he talked with us on the road and opened the Scriptures to us?" (vv. 25-32)

What a poignant depiction of two men walking each other through their distress on the lonely road to Emmaus. What happened on their journey was nothing short of a miracle. Jesus joined them and walked them to the village. Scripture says that as Jesus reminded them of the prophesies about the Messiah, it caused the hearts of his companions to "burn within them." Perhaps it was that divine spark inside them that recognized a connection with their Savior. After all, they were, as God's children, his family.

We can only imagine the joy these followers of Jesus experienced when they finally recognized their Lord as they shared a meal together. By walking them down the road to Emmaus, Jesus helped them remember. He restored their faith and gave them the courage to press on in their calling to share his kingdom community with the world.

Jesus left his followers encouraged and prepared. He had also left them with a promise. When they shared their Last Supper together, Jesus told them, "My Father's house has many rooms; if that were not so, would I have told you that I am going there to prepare a place for you? And if I go and prepare a place for you, I will come back and take you to be with me that you also may be where I am" (John 14:2-3).

As Jesus often did, he spoke in the language of the culture, a language his listeners would understand. With this story, he gave his disciples a telling insight into what he was doing and what was coming.

In Jesus's time, people often lived in large family compounds called *insulae*. Extended families lived together in a series of rooms constructed around a common open courtyard.

According to tradition, when a young man wished to marry a young woman, he would present to her a cup of wine. If she drank from the cup, it meant she accepted his proposal. At this point, the young man would return to his own family's insula, where he and his father would set to work, adding a new room onto the family compound. The material they worked with was stone, so the construction process was a painstaking labor of love.

Once the room was complete, the young man would return to the young woman's insula, marry her, and take his bride home to live with him and his extended family.[14]

In the days and weeks that followed the Passover meal, Jesus's disciples would understand the message of this story. Jesus was indeed making room for them—and for all God's children—in his Father's house, so they could be with him where he was.

Jesus's birth, ministry, suffering, death, and resurrection was the ultimate labor of love for a world lost in darkness. A labor of love that began for us under a shining star in a little town named Bethlehem. A labor of love that came to walk each and every one of us home.

> O holy Child of Bethlehem,
> descend to us, we pray;
> cast out our sin, and enter in,
> be born in us today.
> We hear the Christmas angels
> the great glad tidings tell;
> O come to us, abide with us,
> *our Lord Emmanuel!*[15]

Acknowledgments

Though the idea for this book came suddenly, after awakening from a dream, turning that inspiration into a book was a lengthy endeavor. The process began with a series of Advent sermons I delivered at The Woodlands United Methodist Church. The good people of that congregation have helped me develop as a preacher and pastor for over forty-three years. I am indebted to them for their support and encouragement.

Every book project involves the valuable talents of key people behind the scenes. I want to thank Reverend Kimberly Constant, one of our associate pastors, who helped put structure to my ideas and worked alongside me in developing the sermons. Her talent is significant. I am also grateful for my good friend and writing assistant, Jennifer Wilder Morgan, a gifted author in her own right. Jennifer once more became my partner in a book project. Her creative touch is found throughout the pages of this book as she polishes, improves, and contributes to the content.

Additionally, I would like to express my deep appreciation for the dedicated and skilled people at Abingdon Press. I thank Susan Salley, Associate Publisher of Ministry Resources, who believed in the book concept and encouraged me to go forward, and Maria Mayo, Acquisitions Editor, who kept the project on schedule. Finally, I want to express gratitude to my supportive and loving wife, Beverley, who patiently listened to my thoughts and provided me with valuable feedback.

NOTES

Introduction

1. David H. Stern, *Jewish New Testament Commentary: A Companion Volume to the Jewish New Testament* (Clarksville, MD: Jewish New Testament Publications, 1992), 15.

2. Steve Manskar, "No Holiness But Social Holiness," Discipleship Ministries, The United Methodist Church, November 16, 2015, www.umcdiscipleship.org/blog/no-holiness-but-social-holiness.

3. "John Wesley's Small Groups: Models of Christian Community," *Holiness Today*, November/December 2009, www.holinesstoday.org /john-wesley-small-groups-christian-community.

4. "The Love Feast," Discipleship Ministries, November 14, 2014, www.umcdiscipleship.org/resources/the-love-feast. The quotation is from John Wesley's journal entry for August 8, 1737.

5. Adapted from "Agape feast," Wikipedia, https://en.wikipedia.org/wiki /Agape_feast.

6. "Interview with Tim Chester: Eating with a Mission," Crossway, May 3, 2011, www.crossway.org/articles/interview-with-tim-chester-eating-with -a-mission/.

7. "Interview with Tim Chester."

1. Be a Neighbor

1. George F. Will, "We Have an Epidemic of Loneliness. How Can We Fix It?" *The Washington Post*, October 12, 2018, www.washingtonpost.com /opinions/we-have-an-epidemic-of-loneliness-how-can-we-fix-it/2018 /10/12/e8378a38-cd92-11e8-920f-dd52e1ae4570_story.html.

2. Jenny Anderson, "Loneliness Is Bad for Our Health. Now Governments Around the World Are Finally Tackling It," *Quartz*, October 9, 2018, https://qz.com/1413576/loneliness-is-bad-for-our-health-now -governments-around-the-world-are-finally-tackling-the-problem/.

3. Will, "We Have an Epidemic of Loneliness."

4. C. S. Lewis, *The Weight of Glory*, C. S. Lewis website, www.cslewis.com /be-careful/.

5. C. S. Lewis, *Mere Christianity* (New York: Macmillan, 1996), 116–17.

6. Brett Blair, "No Room in the Inn," Sermons.com, https://sermons.com /sermon/no-room-in-the-inn/1337729.

7. David H. Stern, *Jewish New Testament Commentary: A Companion Volume to the Jewish New Testament* (Clarksville, MD: Jewish New Testament Publications, 1992), 932.

8. Kristin Kerns and L. Slagan Locklear, "Three New Census Bureau Products Show Domestic Migration at Regional, State, and County Levels," United States Census Bureau, April 29, 2019, www.census.gov /library/stories/2019/04/moves-from-south-west-dominate-recent -migration-flows.html.

9. Norman Tokar, dir., *Leave It to Beaver*, season 1, episode 5, "New Neighbors," aired November 1, 1957, on CBS, www.dailymotion.com /video/x4olux6.

10. Edgar A. Guest, *You Can't Live Your Own Life* (Chicago: Reilly and Lee, 1928), 76–77.

11. Bill Bouknight, "Is Someone Knocking," Sermons.com.

12. Mary Foston-English, "Surviving the Family Holiday," BeWell, https://bewell.stanford.edu/surviving-the-family-holiday/.

2. Welcome Strangers

1. Steven Runciman, *A History of the Crusades Vol. 1: The First Crusade and the Foundations of the Kingdom of Jerusalem* (Cambridge, UK: Cambridge University Press, 1951), 10.

2. From "Stranger Danger," copyright © Healthy Start Publishing.

3. Ali Velez, "These 26 Stories About Strangers Helping People in Need Will Remind You That Humanity Is Not Doomed," BuzzFeed, September 9, 2018, www.buzzfeed.com/alivelez/26-stories-about -random-acts-of-kindness-that-will.

4. William Barclay, trans., *The Gospel of Matthew Vol. 1*, *Daily Study Bible* (Philadelphia: Westminster, 1956), 20.

5. James R. Edwards Jr., "A Biblical Perspective on Immigration Policy," Center for Immigration Studies, September 16, 2009, https://cis.org /Report/Biblical-Perspective-Immigration-Policy.

6. Farhat Popal, "Stories from American Immigrants: How Americans Save a Spot at the Table," George W. Bush Presidential Center, October 4, 2017, www.bushcenter.org/publications/articles/2017/10 /immigration-stories-farhat-popal.html.

7. Shelly Bradbury, "A Tiny Colorado Town Opened Its Arms to over 700 Stranded Travelers This Weekend," *The Denver Post*, December 1, 2019, www.denverpost.com/2019/12/01/colorado-road-closures-fairplay -shelters/.

8. Octavio Javier Esqueda, "What's Your Immigration Status? Divine," *Christianity Today*, September 6, 2017, www.christianitytoday.com/ct /2017/september-web-only/jesus-divine-immigration-status-daca.html.

3. Leave the Light On

1. "Star of Bethlehem," *The Cornish Song Book*, ed. Ralph Dunstan (London: Reid Bros., 1929), 111. See www.hymnsandcarolsofchristmas .com/Hymns_and_Carols/star_of_bethlehem2.htm.

2.   Barry Rubin and David Stern, eds., *The Complete Jewish Study Bible: Insights for Jews and Christians* (Peabody, MA: Hendrickson, 2016), 208.

3.   Rubin and Stern, *Complete Jewish Study Bible*, 1384.

4.   Charles Wesley, "Hark! the Herald Angels Sing," *The United Methodist Hymnal* (Nashville: The United Methodist Publishing House, 1989), 240.

5.   Randy Alcorn, "Shepherd's Status," Eternal Perspectives Ministries, March 11, 2008, www.epm.org/resources/2008/Mar/11/shepherds-status/.

6.   Ilan Ben Zion, "Ancient Temple Mount 'Warning' Stone Is 'Closest Thing We Have to the Temple,'" *The Times of Israel*, October 22, 2015, www.timesofisrael.com/ancient-temple-mount-warning-stone-is-closest -thing-we-have-to-the-temple/.

7.   "Helen Keller and Her 'Miracle Worker' Teacher Anne Sullivan," Women You Should Know, October 5, 2018, https://womenyoushould know.net/helen-keller-teacher-anne-sullivan/.

8.   Helen Keller, *The Story of My Life* (Mineola, NY: Dover, 1996), 4.

9.   Corrie ten Boom, *Jesus Is Victor* (Grand Rapids: Revell, 1984), 198.

10. Joseph Mohr, "Silent Night, Holy Night" trans. John F. Young, *The United Methodist Hymnal* (Nashville: The United Methodist Publishing House, 1989), 239.

4. Walk Each Other Home

1.   Phillips Brooks, "O Little Town of Bethlehem," *The United Methodist Hymnal* (Nashville: The United Methodist Publishing House, 1989), 230.

2.   "A Service of Word and Table I and Introductions to the Other Forms: Confession and Pardon," *The United Methodist Book of Worship* (Nashville: The United Methodist Publishing House, 1992), www.umcdiscipleship.org/book-of-worship/a-service-of-word-and-table -i-and-introductions-to-the-other-forms.

3.   Robert D. Putnam, *Bowling Alone: The Collapse and Revival of American Community* (New York: Simon & Schuster, 2000).

4.   John E. Harnish, "A Traveling God in a Pop-Up Camper," Sermons. com, https://sermons.com/sermon/moses-a-traveling-god-in-a-pop-up-camper/1360148.

5.   "In U.S., Decline of Christianity Continues at Rapid Pace," Pew Research Center, October 17, 2019, www.pewforum.org/2019/10/17/in-u-s-decline-of-christianity-continues-at-rapid-pace/.

6.   Tara Isabella Burton, "'Spiritual but Not Religious': Inside America's Rapidly Growing Faith Group," *Vox*, November 10, 2017, www.vox .com/identities/2017/11/10/16630178/study-spiritual-but-not-religious.

7.   "Exploring the Eel River Valley: The Redwood Forest and the Role of Water," Sunny Fortuna, https://sunnyfortuna.com/explore/redwoods _and_water.htm.

8.   Chris Huber, "2017 Hurricane Harvey: Facts, FAQs, and How to Help," World Vision, updated September 7, 2018, www.worldvision.org /disaster-relief-news-stories/2017-hurricane-harvey-facts.

9.   Huber, "2017 Hurricane Harvey."

10. Billy Graham, *Just As I Am: The Autobiography of Billy Graham* (New York: HarperCollins, 1997), 22.

11. Graham, *Just As I Am*, 25.

12. Graham, *Just As I Am*, 29.

13. Laura Bailey, "The Night Billy Graham Was Born Again," Billy Graham Evangelistic Association, November 6, 2017, https://billygraham.org/story/the-night-billy-graham-was-born-again/.

14. Ray Vander Laan, "Insulas," That the World May Know, www.thattheworldmayknow.com/insulas, in Ed Robb, *Mountaintop Moments: Meeting God in the High Places* (Nashville: Abingdon Press, 2019), 88–89.

15. Brooks, "O Little Town of Bethlehem," 230 (emphasis added).